296.311
L53   Lelyveld, Arthur J.
a   Atheism is dead.

296.311
L53   Lelyveld, Arthur J
a   Atheism is dead.

Temple Israel

Library

Minneapolis, Minn.

———

Please sign your full name on the above card.

Return books promptly to the Library or Temple Office.

Fines will be charged for overdue books or for damage or loss of same.

ATHEISM IS DEAD

ATHEISM IS DEAD

A Jewish Response to Radical Theology

ARTHUR J. LELYVELD

THE WORLD PUBLISHING COMPANY
Cleveland and New York

Published by The World Publishing Company
2231 West 110th Street, Cleveland, Ohio 44102

Published simultaneously in Canada by Nelson, Foster & Scott Ltd.

First Printing 1968

Library of Congress Catalog Card Number: 67–18031

PRINTED IN THE UNITED STATES OF AMERICA

FOR TEELA

PREFACE

It may be that the most religious men living today are those who out of profound concern have said that God is dead.

Few of the "radical theologians" are atheists in any sense. None is an atheist in the old, doctrinal sense. They are men who want our affirmations and our practices to be honest and meaningful expressions of contemporary need and modern truth, not meaningless or merely ceremonial culture patterns.

I share their concern, but I believe their formulations to be out of date. They are victims of a culture lag when they take their stand either in empiricism or in language analysis. We are all of us empiricists; but the frontiers of experience have been pushed so far out that our grandfathers' comprehension of the term will be totally inadequate to today's reality. The old arguments about proofs and the debates about concepts have been replaced by discussions of the meaningfulness of depth experiences and the variant roles of language in communicating meaning.

When, therefore, I say that atheism is dead I do not say it as a simplistic or flippant response. I am serious. I say it in the conviction that new knowledge in the physical sciences, as well as in anthropology and psychology, has swept away the preconceptions on which much of the old atheism was based: both mechanism and the naive, self-confident forms of humanism.

We can paraphrase Nietzsche by saying that although atheism is dead the masses of men do not know it; they have not heard the "news" yet.

This book then is more than a response to radical theology.

It is a view of God and religion held by one who considers himself both modern and open; who, if he has blind spots, wants them to be illuminated; who, like the radicals, wants religion to function meaningfully and effectively in the lives of men and in the problems of society. It is written in the belief that the average, intelligent, and concerned individual to whom it is addressed must inevitably be affected by the intellectual struggles of theologians and has, therefore, a right to enter into them.

There is a danger inherent in the complexity of modern life that theology may become an ever more specialized and professionalized discipline that will cease to have meaning for nontheologians. Theology, unhappily, is assuming a professional gloss just as philosophy is beginning to emerge from the limitations that were imposed upon it by positivism in its various forms and by concentration on linguistics. Not being a theologian, I have become engaged as a result of being threatened. I wince when, in response to the pained and earnest announcement, "God is dead," the bumper stickers raucously proclaim, "God is not dead—He is in Acapulco." The derision is invited by the *avant-garde* sensationalism. I feel it is better to be understood than "in"; and I would rather be "square" than wrong.

My intention is to come to grips with essentially human problems—with the role of the person in relation to other persons, to the harsh complexities of modern technology, and to the widening universe in which he has his being. I have written out of the world-view and the stance of a liberal, modern Jew who affirms the covenant role of the people of Israel. My argument, therefore, frequently erupts in that ancient form known as apologetics and polemics. We call it "dialogue" today.

But if I argue and debate, it is not because I do not wish to listen—listening is the prime responsibility for anyone engaged in dialogue. Rather, I have tried to state my position as strongly as possible both in order to clarify it and in order to elicit a response.

The problems of contemporary theology are far more difficult for Christianity than they are for Judaism. It might be said that the death-of-God theologians wait for God while embracing the Messiah, whereas normative Judaism has always embraced God while striving to *bring* the Messiah. We are not burdened by the problems of Christology. But we are not immune from this situation.

The urban setting is not new to us, but we must labor within it. We do not have the problem of John Robinson with the "three-layer cake" universe. Long ago Job asked, "Will you tell lies on behalf of God?" We have known throughout our history an insistent demand for integrity even in our verbalizations. But we may very well be affected by a world in which the affirmations that have been central for us are no longer viable for the great masses of men. Judaism cannot survive in a religionless or posthumanistic era.

Because we are endangered by this situation, it is well that we respond to it and seek to understand it. We do so recognizing that Judaism has something to contribute to the dialogue. The prophets have spoken in a Judaic sense to Christianity again and again in Christian history. Much of the contemporary radical Christian emphasis on man in society, much of the modern return to the Social Gospel, to the emphasis on civil rights, and to world peace by the Christian clergy can be said to represent a Judaizing tendency—more power to it!

The Jews prays that when the Lord shall be king over all the earth, the Lord shall be one and His name shall be one. The recent Vatican Council statement says that the Church awaits that day, known to God alone, on which all peoples will address the Lord in a single voice and serve him shoulder to shoulder. And Martin Buber ends his reverent study of the gospels, of the difference between Christian faith and Jewish faith, with this statement: "The faith of Judaism, the faith of Christendom are by nature different in kind, each in conformity with its human basis, and they will indeed remain different, until mankind is gathered in from the exiles of the 'religions' into the Kingship of God. But an Israel striving after the renewal of its faith through the rebirth of the person and a Christianity striving for the renewal of its faith through the rebirth of nations would have something as yet unsaid to say to each another and a help to give to one another—hardly to be conceived at the present time." *

Both in our respective liturgies and in Martin Buber this reconciliation will take place at the *end* of days. In the interim, we must talk to one another, not to seek homogenization of our differing faiths, but to learn from one another, to understand one another, and to respond to a common situation of anguish and of expectation.

Not least among the positive results of the radical proclamations has been the stimulation of new interest in the intellectual problems of religion. Indeed, this book owes its coming into being at this moment to the writings of the death-of-God thinkers, and it might well be gratefully dedicated to them were it not that there is one who is much more directly responsible for it. My gratitude and love go, therefore, in greatest measure to her, Teela Lelyveld, my wife, who encouraged it and made it possible. My thanks are due as well to my colleagues, Rabbi Earl Jordan and Rabbi Barry Friedman, who were unfailingly helpful; to Saul S. Spiro, mentor and friend from whom I have learned much Torah; to Bess Rosenfeld, the librarian of Fairmount Temple, who carted books and checked references; to Gertrude Resnick, my secretary, who skillfully engineered innumerable details; and to Ben and Robin, who frequently made room about me so that I could work. My son, Joseph Lelyveld, gave the manuscript a responsible and rigorously critical reading. Most of his suggestions have been incorporated into the text; our continuing disagreements will, I hope, be the subject of affectionate debate for years to come. My loving thanks go also to my sons, David Lelyveld, who made many constructive comments on the manuscript, and Michael, whose rejection of its point of view was chastening and salutary. None of those who have freely helped me bear any responsibility for the book;

* Martin Buber, *Two Types of Faith* (New York: The Macmillan Company, 1951), pp. 173–174.

for while I hope it is solidly grounded in reason and in historic Judaism, it is essentially a statement of personal conviction which must stand or fall by its own inner integrity and the measure of its persuasiveness.

A. J. L.

Cleveland, Ohio
October, 1967

BIBLIOGRAPHICAL NOTE

My indebtedness to a host of writers and scholars is, I hope, amply attested in the footnotes; my primary debt to the thought of the late Martin Buber could not be adequately annotated but should be apparent to all who know his work.

In rendering the Hebrew Bible, I have for the most part relied on the 1917 translation of the Jewish Publication Society of America (Philadelphia). Where I depart from this version, it is because I have supplied my own translation in the effort to penetrate the direct meaning of the Hebrew text. For the New Testament citations, I have relied exclusively on the Revised Standard Version (New York: Thomas Nelson and Sons, 1953).

The translation of rabbinic material is generally my own except where a specific translation is cited. Where reference is made to *the* Talmud, it is the Babylonian Talmud that is meant: namely, that huge corpus of rabbinic thought that was completed in Babylonia about the year 500 C.E. In each instance in which I quote this Talmud, I give a page reference to the so-called "Soncino" translation. This monumental translation embracing thirty-four volumes plus a large index volume was completed in England in 1952 under the editorship of Rabbi Dr. I. Epstein (London: The Soncino Press, 1938–1952). These page references are primarily for the convenience of the reader who is unable to refer to the original Hebrew; I have not hesitated to supply my own translation where I have found it necessary to do so in order to get at the sense of the Hebrew or the Aramaic text. These comments also apply to the "Soncino translation" of the *Midrash Rabba* (ed. Rabbi Dr. H. Freedman and Maurice Simon. London: The Soncino Press, 1939). In my citation of general rabbinical works which are not available in English translation, I give no publishing data except in those few instances where there are definitive editions. The Jerusalem Talmud, completed in Palestine about the year 400 C.E., is in this category of works unavailable in English and for which the traditional mode of reference familiar to Hebrew scholars is used. I have tried to be consistent and at the same time simple in my transliteration of the Hebrew words, using the Sephardic pronunciation currently in use in Israel.

A. J. L.

CONTENTS

Proem

It is said of Levi Yitzchok, the beloved Chassidic saint who lived in Berdichev in the second half of the eighteenth century and who was known as The Berdichever Rebbe, that one busy market day he sent his *shammes,* or beadle, to summon all his *balebatim,* all the substantial Jews of his community, to an emergency meeting. Trembling with concern, they came running from their crafts and trades—for if their *rebbe* had called them to come together in the midst of a day when they were steeped in the business of this world it must surely be a matter of extreme urgency. They knew Levi Yitzchok to be gentle and forebearing. They knew that he had been disturbed about ethical lapses in the community. They knew above all his love and his concern for human beings. And so they hurried to answer his summons. The rabbi entered the room and they were immediately silent. "My people," the rabbi said, "I have called you together to make a very important announcement." They hung on his words. "This is the announcement," he continued. He paused. Then firmly, indeed dramatically, he declared: *"There is a God in the world."* And, slowly, the rabbi turned and walked out of the room.

PART ONE

THE ATTACKING FORCES

But wherefore could not I pronounce "Amen"?
I had most need of blessing, and "Amen"
Stuck in my throat.

Shakespeare, *Macbeth*

CHAPTER ONE

THE ECHO OF NIETZSCHE

The phrase "God is dead" is a metaphorical expression and intentionally so. Those who use it seek to shock—while expressing what they see as a fact of our time. They mean that the concept of God has ceased to function, or that it is no longer meaningful, or that nothing exists to which the word "God" can be applied, that there is no reality to which it can point.

"God is dead" as a literal statement would be a nonsense proposition at this stage of human cultural development. The common consent of sophisticated men has long recognized the word "God," however interpreted or received, to mean at least the ultimate source or the ultimate nature of all that exists. Our culture in its literary and philosophical expression has long been monotheistic. The idea of a "dying god" was possible only in those mythologies that affirmed a plurality of forces governing nature and the life of man. Tammuz and Adonis, Attis and Osiris, Dionysus and Persephone, could in the cycles of the seasons undergo death and resurrection as in the Temperate Zones all vegetation withered in the fall and burgeoned in the spring.[1] The word "god" as it functioned in such mythologies is certainly no longer intellectually viable except in poetic or historical contexts.

The *whole* metaphor has nontheless been embraced by many of those who "do theology" [2] in the "death of God" style today and who speak of awaiting God's reappearance or resurrection.

[1] See Sir James George Frazer, *The New Golden Bough,* ed. Theodore H. Gaster (New York: Criterion Books, 1959), Part IV, pp. 208–302.

[2] See William H. Hamilton and Thomas J. J. Altizer, *Radical Theology and the Death of God* (Indianapolis: The Bobbs-Merrill Company, Inc., 1966), p. 6.

Some of them who are still labeled theologians, but who are more properly called "nontheologians" or "a-theologians," believe that modern philosophy has made the use of any "God-language" impossible. The very terminology they use—for example, their references to "style" and "doing theology"—reveals the professionalism of their stance, a gloss that may make their "anguish" less anguished and more acceptable to the intellectual. William Hamilton bravely says ". . . we do not know, do not adore, do not possess, do not believe in God . . . We are not talking about the absence of the experience of God, but about the experience of the absence of God." [3] He qualifies this assertion, however, with a "provisional summary" in which he states, ". . . the death of God must be affirmed; the confidence with which we thought we could speak of God is gone, and our faith, belief, experience of him are very poor things indeed . . . Our waiting for God, our godlessness, is partly a search for a language and a style by which we might be enabled to stand before him once again, delighting in his presence." [4]

The "experience of God's absence" is not new in religious thought. It is to be found in Biblical religion. The Psalmist speaks in another metaphor when he challenges God, saying, "How long wilt Thou hide Thy face from me?";[5] and Martin Buber has dealt perceptively and effectively with the Nietzschean assertion of God's death with the metaphor, "eclipse of God," suggesting that there is that in the modern world which has interposed itself between man and God, leaving man in friendless darkness.[6]

The proclamation "God is dead!" is not new, either. It was given its most vigorous expression by the late nineteenth-century German thinker and writer, that compelling and tortured genius, Friedrich Nietzsche. What Nietzsche meant is not easily stated,

[3] Hamilton and Altizer, pp. 26, 28.

[4] Hamilton and Altizer, p. 41.

[5] In Psalm 13:1; cf. Psalm 10:1, 89:46, and Deuteronomy 31:17 f., 32:20.

[6] Martin Buber, *Eclipse of God: Studies in the Relation Between Religion and Philosophy* (New York: Harper & Brothers, 1952), especially pp. 20–24.

for Nietzsche was not a systematic thinker. He was impulsive, emotional, poetic—and hence he meant many things—different meanings at different moments.

In Nietzsche, the "death of God" is a rhetorical device, a piece of vivid imagery that conveys both Nietzsche's atheism and his contempt for those who have "killed" God, his pain of loss, and his exultation in new freedom. The fatuousness of man, his narrow joylessness and "alien" sense of sin, have closed his ears to the epochal news.

The old gods did not simply fade away. They came to a rollicking end "long ago" laughing themselves to death:

> ... verily, they had a good gay godlike end. They did not end in a "twilight," though this lie is told.[7] Instead: One day they *laughed* themselves to death. That happened when the most godless word issued from one of the gods themselves—the word: "There is one god. Thou shalt have no other god before me!" An old grimbeard of a god, a jealous one, thus forgot himself. And then all the gods laughed and rocked on their chairs and cried, "Is not just this godlike that there are gods but no God?" [8]

Now the very god who had caused the other gods to laugh themselves to death is also dead, says Nietzche. In *The Gay Science,* in 1882, Nietzsche had broached this idea by portraying a madman who calls out in the market place, "I seek God." All the unbelievers, of whom there were many, mock him and laugh at him, until the madman chills them with the accusation that men have murdered God. They have lost all sources of direction and meaning and cannot as yet understand what the death of God means for human history:

> Do we not dash on unceasingly? Backwards, sideways, forwards, in all directions? Is there still an above and below? Do we not stray, as through infinite nothingness? Does not empty space breathe upon us? Has it not become colder? Does not night come on continually, darker and darker? Shall we not have to light

7 A reference to Richard Wagner's opera *Götterämmerung.*

8 Friedrich Nietzsche, *Thus Spoke Zarathustra,* in *The Portable Nietzsche,* trans. and ed. Walter Kaufmann (New York: The Viking Press, 1954), Part III, p. 294.

lanterns in the morning? Do we not hear the noise of the grave-
diggers who are burying God? Do we not smell the divine putre-
faction?—For even gods putrefy. God is dead! God remains
dead! And we have killed him. . . . Shall we not ourselves have
to become gods, merely to seem worthy of it? There never was
a greater event,—and on account of it, all who are born after us
belong to a higher history than any history hitherto! [9]

But men are slow to understand, Nietzsche laments. Churches
still function even though they are now only tombs and monu-
ments of the dead God. Therefore, it becomes Zarathustra's task
to spread the word, and Zarathustra comes down from the
mountains. He encounters an old man—a "holy man" and a
"saint"—who tells him that he loves God but loves not man,
for man is too imperfect. Nietzsche then has Zarathustra embrace the other end of this unnecessary dichotomy and declare,
"I love man." Zarathustra asks the saint what he is doing in
the forest. "I make songs and sing them," says the old man;
"and when I make songs, I laugh, cry and hum: thus I praise
God." Then Zarathustra and the old man laugh together "as two
boys laugh." When they have separated, Zarathustra asks himself, "Could it be possible? This old saint in the forest has not
yet heard anything of this, that *God is dead!*" [10]

Nietzsche's presentation of the death of God can be defined
in terms that have come to be known as "existentialist." The
statement "God is dead" is a protest announcement that the old
theistic fount of meaning no longer flows. But man has entered
a new phase of history—now the Superman or "Overman" must
emerge.[11] Nietzsche is thus calling on man to create his own
meaning by living as nobly as possible within the situation in
which he finds himself.

Two aspects of Nietzsche's point of view must be recognized

---

[9] No. 125, *The Complete Works of Friedrich Nietzsche* (New York:
The Macmillan Company, 1924), X, 168. (Titled here "The Joyful
Wisdom.")

[10] Kaufmann's translation, *Thus Spoke Zarathustra*, Part I, p. 123.
The emphasis is Nietzsche's. See *Also Sprach Zarathustra* (Stuttgart:
Alfred Kroner Verlag, 1950), p. 8.

[11] *Ibid., loc. cit.*

if we are to understand his position and his mood. First, Nietzsche was an atheist, and his atheism is philosophically grounded. "God is a conjecture," he tells us. The statement is reiterated several times in *Thus Spoke Zarathustra.* What is more, he says, this conjecture is an unfruitful one, inadequate to man's needs. Conjectures, he tells us, should not reach beyond man's creative will and should be limited by what is thinkable.[12]

The second aspect is a matter of tone. Despite the painful critical context out of which it arises, the Nietzschean proclamation has a triumphant ring. The new era of history that recognition of God's death will initiate will also release man from bondage. It is a proclamation that looks to the future. God is dead—; Long live the *Übermensch!* For this Overman is to be God's successor. He is the fulfilled and independent Man who rejects the "morality of slaves," overturns the scale of values, rejecting the old namby-pamby morality, and embraces the "morality of masters." In Part V of *The Gay Science,* which he wrote as an addendum in 1887, Nietzsche describes "the background" of his "cheerfulness":

> The greatest recent event—that "God is dead," that the belief in the Christian God has ceased to be believable—is even now beginning to cast its first shadows over Europe. . . . We philosophers and "free spirits" feel as if a new dawn were shining on us when we receive the tidings that "the old god is dead," our heart overflows with gratitude, amazement, anticipation, expectation.[13]

True, the horizon is not altogether bright. We have not emancipated ourselves from "morality"; we are still pious. We still have a "will to truth," and this may interfere with that unbridled "will to power" that alone can fully emancipate us. And what we must be emancipated *from,* is Christianity—a "faith" that is a "veto against science," that is "mortally" hostile against the "wisdom of this world," and that is filled with errors that are "thoroughly Jewish." [14]

[12] Kaufmann's translation, *Thus Spoke Zarathustra,* Part II, pp. 197, 198.
[13] Kaufmann's translation, pp. 447, 448.
[14] Kaufmann's translation, *The Antichrist,* p. 627.

Here we see how Nietzsche provided one of the strands of twentieth-century paganism as well as the background for turn-of-the-century Scientism, a faith that science and technology would soon bring complete freedom to the human race. The mood of Nietzsche's "God is dead!" is in harmony with Algernon Swinburne's doxology in "The Hymn of Man":

> Glory to Man in the highest!
> For Man is the master of things.

This mood is gone—it is effectively *dead,* except where a culture lag has closed men's ears to the news as much as their ears were closed to the earlier "news" brought by Nietzsche. If the harrowing events of our own century have not wholly shattered our confidence, they have at least moderated our ebullience. *"Hubris,"* swollen human pride and self-confidence, was in Greek drama the prelude to the confrontation with Nemesis. We may welcome the new uncertainties in religion and the new humilities in science as hopeful signs.

It is therefore a strange and unexpected turn when, as an act of supreme sensationalism or extreme despair, a new and apodictic pronouncement of God's death is made from one segment of the ramparts of the citadels of religion. At least, it would seem to the general public that this echo of the Nietzschean epitaph is being pronounced with absolute certainty by the "God-is-dead" theologians. Were they truly certain, we would think them far behind the times. Actually, they are neither triumphant nor flip. Their pronouncements grow out of a genuine anxiety and a genuine concern with basic philosophical problems.

Their genuineness does not, however, make them immune from criticism and challenge. And just as Mark Twain announced that the news of his death had been "greatly exaggerated," so it may well be that this belated second announcement of the death of God is a gross exaggeration.

What must be challenged in contemporary radical theology is the consistency and the meaningfulness of the variant for-

mulations and conclusions. The mood of inquiry and the manifestation of integrity that motivates them are welcome allies in
the quest for religious truth. Anguish and doubt are perennial
aspects of that quest. "I believe; help my unbelief!" [15] has been
the cry of men of all traditions. Tennyson's paradox of the faith
that lives in honest doubt is part of the experience of those who
conscientiously probe for meaning and who frequently know
"God's absence."

The experience of God's absence was certainly not uncommon in the history of the Jewish people—a people who have
known pogrom and rack, exile and repression almost without
surcease. Usually, the Jew looks within himself and examines
his deeds in order to find the reason for that absence. "Because
of our sins," says the prayerbook in bold self-assumption of
responsibility, "we were exiled from our land." [16]

For Buber, the eclipse of God takes place in the "between-
ness" of the relationship between man and God. It is not necessarily the result of anything done by man, and it is certainly
not in anything happening in "the Eternal Thou who lives on
in the light of His eternity" even during the eclipse. Elsewhere
in Jewish thought, however, God's absence is viewed as the
result of man's failures in his conduct toward his fellows—not
as a result of inadequate speculation nor because a new language
or a new style in theology is needed.

"Thus taught the sages," we read in an old rabbinic work,[17]
"thy deeds will bring thee near [to God] and thy deeds will remove thee [from God]. How so? If a man does ugly things his
actions remove him from the divine presence . . ." and they
cite as the proof text these verses from Isaiah 59:

[15] Mark 9:24.

[16] See the Talmud. Tractate *Sotah* 3b. (Soncino translation, p. 11).
". . . before Israel sinned the *Shechinah* (Divine presence) abode with
each individual; . . . when they sinned, the *Shechinah* departed from
them."

[17] *Seder Eliyahu*, ed. Friedmann (Vienna: 1900), p. 104. Quoted by
Solomon Schechter in *Some Aspects of Rabbinic Theology* (New York:
The Macmillan Company, 1909), pp. 233, 33.

Behold, the Lord's hand is not shortened, that
    it cannot save,
Neither is His ear heavy, that it cannot hear;
but your iniquities have separated
    you and your God,
And your sins have hid his face from you
    That he will not hear.
For your hands are defiled with blood
and your fingers with iniquity;
Your lips have spoken lies. . . .

The phrase "God lives!" it must be said, is just as metaphorical as "God is dead!" It is the antithesis of the Nietzschean proclamation; the response of affirmation. It testifies to the experience of God's presence. A statement of faith—as is its opposite—it proclaims that this total and complex process in which we are involved has significance and that the recognition of its significance is accessible to man. It means to say that there is that which undergirds, encompasses, and fills all-that-is, which gives meaning and coherence to all-that-is. When we say "God lives" we mean that those who are attentive to the address of the Whole will know God's presence and will find it possible to stand in relationship to Him. When we say "God lives" we mean that man is capable of responding to that ultimate Demand that speaks from the reality of all-that-is and that he is capable of participating in the fulfillment of its meaning. We mean that the experience of demand and response with its coordinate responsibility is one of the empirical facts of human experience, a fact that man must seek to understand in its deepest significance.

In using the phrase, all-that-is, we are deliberately seeking to avoid the dualisms of traditional speculation: matter and spirit, extension and thought, natural and supernatural. These crutches are ever more clearly exposed as evidences of that unequal race in which discovery always outstrips philosophical adjustment. The new science tells us with increasing reliability and certainty that the cosmos, the Whole within which we have our being, is truly a universe. The same formulas that describe the minuscule relationships in the world of particles and nuclear physics will ultimately be found to describe relationships in the Macrocosm, the vast reaches of intergalactic space, as well.

All that *is,* is *natural.* In that totality of being, there are aspects accessible to our limited intelligence, and there are others that are not. But that which is not accessible to us is no less "natural" than that which is.

When we affirm that "God lives" we try to see through our failures, our incompleteness and our partial knowledge, we aspire to penetrate the fragmentary and the changing and to confront the eternal unity that informs all existence. We seek the abiding truths that condition all human striving.

We must not mistake the *words,* "God lives," for the reality that they are intended to evoke. Nor should we be put off by the traditional clothing of the expression. The stance of which I am speaking, and of which "God is dead" is the denial, is one that can be given a rich variety of linguistic garments. Essentially, it is the persistent and courageous affirmation that existence is meaningful and that man's life has meaning in the context of existence—not merely a meaning man himself invents and infuses into it but an ultimate and essential meaning for which he is bound to quest.

This is a stance that is far more than a gesture of loyalty to ancient faith or a stubborn response to those who attack it. It is the critical test of modern man in a human situation that threatens to destroy all those values we have come to know as "humane" or, indeed, to terminate the human episode. "God lives!" is a battle cry in the struggle against philosophies of despair, in the war against all those trends that would depersonalize man, reduce him to a statistic or a numbered cog in a machine-governed antlike society of function and effect. It is this threat, to which we now turn our attention, that makes the proclamation of God's death a crucial challenge. "God is dead" is a dramatic proclamation of man's anguish. "God lives!" is a proclamation that seeks the survival of man as man.

CHAPTER TWO

WHAT IS HAPPENING TO MAN?

Most men, whatever their verbal affirmations, are practicing atheists. In this sense, God is truly dead for them. This is what it means to say the death of God is a cultural fact. More and more, man is being ridden by what he has created. He may be the "maker," but he is losing out as the "master" of things. When expediency rules him, when he takes his directions from his "situation" or his peers, then in practical terms, he denies God.

Atheism is not the new factor in our human situation. Through our entire cultural history, we have known those who reject God and the God-idea. We find them in the Bible—the "fool" described by the Psalmists: "The fool has said in his heart, 'There is no God!' " [1] We find him in classical philosophy—typified in Epicurus, who rejected the idea that "the gods" stand in any meaningful relationship to men and who proclaimed the independence of men from any divine interference. Man must find by his own efforts both pleasure and nobility within his brief life, which is his only life. Epicurus is in some respects a Roman forerunner of contemporary existentialists.

Atheists in the old Jewish milieu were always of this stamp— they said, "There is no judgment and there is no Judge," [2] and they meant that there exists no absolute source of good and

---

[1] Psalms 14:1 and 53:1. Note in the following verse how this "fool" is identified. He does corrupt, abominable deeds. He denies God silently—"in his heart"—but proclaims his atheism by his actions.

[2] Genesis Rabba, XXVI:6, citing Psalm 10:13 as a proof text. (This is part of a collection of sermonic materials related to the first five books of the Bible, called the *Midrash Rabba* and compiled between the fourth and twelfth centuries of the Christian Era.) Soncino translation, p. 217.

evil, no tribunal, personal or impersonal, by which they might be judged. It is interesting to note that the Hebrew term applied to the atheist linked him to the Epicureans and was not altogether incorrect in that linkage. He was called an *"apikoros."* But the *"apikoros"* is more a skeptic and scoffer than an atheist. The closest the Hebrew language comes to "atheist" is the phrase *"kofer b'ikkar,"* the one who "denies the root." However, his denial is also generated by his conduct and becomes evident in his conduct:

> A "philosopher" is said to have asked Rabbi Reuben in Tiberias, Who is the most hateful man in the world? The rabbi replied, "He who denies his creator." To the question how that was, he answered by reciting the commandments, Honor thy father and thy mother, thou shalt not kill, thou shalt not commit adultery, and so on to the end of the Decalogue, continuing, "No man denies the obligation of one of those commandments until he *denies the root* [my emphasis] . . . and no man goes and commits a transgression unless he has first denied Him who laid the command upon him." [3]

The entire context of this anecdote is interesting, for it grows out of a discussion of several verses in the Book of Leviticus where deceiving one's neighbor is regarded as committing a trespass against God. [4]

It is this practical atheist who is regarded in Jewish thought as a menace to mankind: the man who by his actions demonstrates that he has rejected or despised the divine demand made upon him. For God is encountered first as the source of demand—by Abraham the progenitor of the Jewish people, when he receives a commission, "Get thee out . . . And be thou a bless-

---

[3] As quoted by George Foot Moore, *Judaism* (Cambridge, Mass.: Harvard University Press, 1932), I, 467; see also I, 360, and notes thereto. Tosefta *Sh'vuot* III:5 [not III:6, as cited in Moore]: "No man denies his neighbor (deals fraudulently with him) until he denies the root." (The *Tosefta* is a post-third-century compilation of material parallel to the *Mishnah*, which in turn is the organized presentation of rabbinic traditions through the close of the second century, and itself constitutes the core of the Talmud.)

[4] Leviticus 5:21-24.

ing" [5]—and by the primal pair, "Be fruitful and multiply . . .
replenish the earth and subdue it." [6] Only later does He become
the other pole of a crucial and supportive relationship—and
much later, the object of speculation. The frequently quoted
Talmudic aphorism, "Would that they had forsaken Me and
kept my Torah," makes this progression clear, for it adds the
phrase (less frequently quoted) "because the light of the Torah
will bring them near to Me." [7]

It is this *practicing* atheist—denying God by ignoring His
demands—who abounds in modern times. The polls assure us
that 97 per cent to 99 per cent of the American people affirm
a "belief in God." Yet no earnest observer would maintain that
this belief *functions* effectively in the lives of most Americans,
or that fraud, bigotry, lack of concern for neighbor, or selfish
preoccupation with the acquisition of possessions are confined
to one to three per cent of the population. When conduct does
not accord with affirmation, it is as if there had never been any
affirmation. Indeed, it is the very meaninglessness of contemporary affirmations that fosters those dissatisfactions leading to
proclamations of the "death of God." When men say "God,"
clinging to the ceremonial prayer on state occasions or the formal
pronouncement, and the saying has no impact on men's lives,
then God is, so far as humanity and human institutions are concerned, dead. The contrary is, of course, equally correct. Men
may deny God verbally yet follow that vision of human relationship and that concept of human dignity that the high religions
have associated with the divine demand. When they do so, then
for all *practical* purposes, God lives. The test lies not in verbal
formulation but in the experienced relationship to that demand.

The focus of our concern is "practical atheism," the rejection
of humane values, the exploitation of persons, the exaltation of
technological efficiency and technical order over human values

[5] Genesis 12:1-2.
[6] Genesis 1:28.
[7] Jerusalem Talmud, *Chagigah* 1:7. (*Torah,* literally "teaching," refers
primarily to the Pentateuch. Here, it obviously means the whole range
of God's demands.)

and human purposes. Future developments in the human situation will be determined by the nature of man's response to ultimate reality. The fear that is implicit in this discussion grows out of the crisis character of our time—a time of decision-making in which the crucial choices that must be made for man's survival are ultimate in character.

The major fact of our time is the bomb. Whether we speak of it or whether it looms silently over us, it is the context of our thought and action, and it colors our responses. The possibility of what State Department leaders euphemistically call a "nuclear exchange" is more than technological. A "nuclear exchange" is an everyday, actual possibility. The picture of its potential consequences is intolerable to the normal mind. Indeed, it is only by masking or blocking out those consequences that we can soberly discuss our graduation from megatons to gigatons and can consider our ability to construct a weapon that, orbiting, unseen and unheard, one hundred miles above our heads, could at any moment blast, scorch, and annihilate an area as large as our entire country—only one step away from the Doomsday Machine, the ultimate weapon horrendously projected by the scientific imagination as being well within our power to construct. This is the frame of reference that brings a new, piercing quality to Paul Valéry's wry comment that "the future, like everything else, is no longer quite what it used to be"—although what he called a "crisis of the unforeseen" is now a "crisis of the foreseen."

The bomb is both fact and symbol. It not only threatens us; it also dramatizes the radical nature of the changes spawned by the last quarter century. The comfortable old categories of thought are irrelevant, for the bomb and all that it represents have introduced into our situation what Karl Jaspers rightfully calls "a new dimension." Not only has it afforded us, for the first time, the capacity to destroy ourselves completely, but it epitomizes the incredible and unprecedented acceleration of change in which it is both product and precipitant. The creator—for the present, the master—of that change is man's scientific discovery and its technological application. We accept the pro-

priety of men orbiting the earth at more than 17,000 miles per
hour for no other reason than that they can, just as Sir Edmund
Hillary and others have climbed Mount Everest because "it is
there." Landing a man on the moon is a commonplace technological probability even though we have not as yet elaborated
in all its detail our rationalization of why we *should* seek to land
a man on the moon. Automation proceeds at a relentlessly increasing pace despite our inadequate preparation for the social
and spiritual adjustments it will require. Meanwhile, half the
world starves slowly, and populations explode unministered to
by our scientific skills. This looming possibility of self-destruc-
tion makes our age different from prior ages: a quantitative
difference resulting from increased technological capacities and
affecting qualitatively the total pattern of our lives.

The new instruments in men's hands do not, however, tell the
entire story. Another aspect of the difference between today and
yesterday bears directly on the problem of our relationship to
God. In the past, destructive and dividing forces were in conflict with a powerful counterforce, an accepted structure of
meaning within which they were characterized as evil. It may
have been a primitive structure in which men had to struggle
against animistic forces that were sometimes beneficent and
frequently malign. Within that structure, there was an inhibiting
fear of punishment for the violation of taboos. More highly developed structures may have posited a conflict between equally
powerful gods, with man forced to choose his position in the
cosmic battle. More recently, the structure included a conception of a divine plan within which man's vocation and obligation were clearly stipulated. In every instance, evil operated
within—and was at least partly contained by—a context. Men
did not always behave well—indeed they most often behaved
very badly—but they knew guilt and amendment, and they drew
from their world-view a supportive meaning and direction.

Our own culture is floundering. It is the heir of two structures
of meaning, both of which are present in our traditions and our
verbal affirmations, but neither of which elicits the confidence
of modern man. One is the structure of traditional Western reli-

gion; the other is the substitute religion of Humanism. The certainty of a divine plan that defined man's role began to lose its intellectual props with the development of philosophical skepticism. Closely allied to the development of scientific method, a line of thought gathered power during the eighteenth and nineteenth centuries that made *doubt* the touchstone of man's response to his world and exalted as the sole measure of truth the process of subjecting propositions to the test of experience. This line goes from Descartes and Hume through Comte to Wittgenstein and through William James to John Dewey. Its differentiated subdivisions bear various names: empiricism, with its focus in the rigid analysis of experience; positivism; pragmatism—the testing by results; naturalism; and instrumentalism. But they all agree that the search for an "absolute," or a set of meanings beyond the actual processes that can be analyzed by sense experience, is a search for a black cat in a dark room at midnight. The cat is not there. The great systematizers who continued to look for a structure of meaning—pre-eminent among them Kant, Hegel, and Marx—were unable to stand up under the pounding analysis of that line whose major thrust was that there is no structure of meaning beyond that which man can supply out of the given world of facts.

This may seem far away from the thinking of "ordinary men"—those without philosophical training or interest—but ordinary men are not unaffected by what goes on in the studies of the intellectuals. In this instance, the penetrating and disturbing analyses of brilliant thinkers created a climate of thought that the already tottering traditional structure of meaning could not weather. Those who accepted the conclusion that there was no possibility of finding meaning in the Whole could react in one of two ways: They could feel a release of pride and confidence in man, who now would grapple unaided with the world that is given to him—this was the line of Humanism—or they could adopt a negative complex of despair and anxiety in confronting the absurdity of man's fate—this was the line of existentialism.

The seeds of both Humanism and existentialism can be found in Nietzsche, who, as we have seen, envisioned the Overman's

mastery of his world but saw him alone, holding total responsibility for his decisions amidst the paradoxes of existence. From
his thought and from the later influences of an earlier thinker—
the strange, proleptic writings of Søren Kierkegaard, a Dane
who had already lived and written in the first half of the nineteenth century—one can move through the line of intellectual
development to such influential contemporary thinkers as Martin
Heidegger and Jean Paul Sartre, whose starting point in their
response to man's place in the universe is an acceptance of the
absurdity of the total context.

Those who responded affirmatively—whom we may lump together as humanists—found a new structure of meaning, the
one under which we still *operate* in our world today even though
our confidence in it has been gravely shaken. They found meaning in man, whose technological and scientific competence
would, they believed, soon give him an all-inclusive competence.
He would empirically solve all his problems, build with his scientific skill a world of peace and justice, even establish empirically a science of values that would support harmony and
good will and make possible an ordered, democratic society in
which human happiness would be ensured. They sang with Tennyson of the "Parliament of man," of "Men, my brothers, men
the workers, ever reaping something new: That which they have
done but earnest of the things that they shall do."

The mood even of those who cling to a humanist outlook is
somewhat more sober today. The events of our time have chill-
ingly underscored man's limitations. Two World Wars climax-
ing in horrible mass destruction of noncombatants by atomic
power; the systematic extermination of European Jewry, with
the death in concentration camps and gas chambers of some
6,000,000 men, women, and children, who were shoveled into
mass graves and crematories; the persistence of tyranny, the
repression of freedom in the arts and sciences, and the denial of
human rights in the Soviet Union, to which millions looked a
quarter century ago as the promising "motherland of socialism";
the survival of hatred, class distinctions, racial discrimination,

and poverty in the democracies—all have tarnished the bright vision prevailing at the turn of the century.

We no longer believe that science will solve all our problems. Those who exalted science as a god in a religion of "scientism" are coming to understand that science is a tool—an exceedingly valuable and perhaps even determinative instrument in the evolutionary process—but, nonetheless, a tool, which may serve for evil as well as for good, for destruction and division as well as for development and progress.

Two faiths have lost their power. The movers of men no longer look upon the world as the stage for the drama of salvation. The masses of men are no longer confident that the mastery of things will bring them happiness. The result is uncertainty and that cautious manipulation of things that reflects the weighing of conflicting expediencies rather than the pursuit of commanding goals.

Our situation may be expressed in an analogy that takes the form of a bitter jest. We are, it can be said, like passengers in a great, supersonic air transport. We are seated in our soft, padded chairs, seat belts unfastened, relaxing, reading, working at our papers, playing games, or whiling away the journey in one way or another. Suddenly, the crackling of the amplifiers alerts us for an announcement, and the smooth voice of the pilot is heard: "This is your captain speaking from the flight deck," it says. "We are cruising at an altitude of 36,000 feet and our cabin is pressurized to the equivalent of 4,000 feet above sea level. I have some information which I feel I should share with you. Something has happened to our communications system and we have lost contact with the ground. I am afraid we are off course and we are rapidly running out of fuel. However, I am pleased to say that we are making excellent time!"

If we have lost our way and there is nothing we can do about it, we have no choice but to make peace with the inevitable and function as well as we can within the limited situation that is given to us. But although we no longer have a clear sense of direction, it is not altogether certain that there is nothing we can do about it. We can, at the very least, make every effort to get our compasses working again.

Our anxiety, our alienation, and our confusion, our sense of being "stranger and afraid in a world we never made," have increased in direct proportion to our loss of conviction about the purpose and meaning of our lives. People are unable to live without a frame of reference, psychologist Wolfgang Köhler tells us, and so they turn to ersatz meanings such as exaggerated worship of the State.[8] The *"Krise der Wissenschaft,"* as Köhler calls it, the "crisis of scholarship," inheres in the fact that scholars have retired into their own little realm of fact and have left questions of value and meaning, questions of moral and metaphysical import, unsolved.

They shunt their values onto a siding while the demands of expediency get a clear track. Or they themselves follow the perilous single track of their own preoccupation. One of the issues of the postwar *Bulletin of Atomic Scientists* [9] contained a reflection that in context was not intended to be humorous or cynical but was soberly included in a sober report. It said: "The area that can be poisoned with fission products available to us today is disappointingly small."

The scientist who wrote that statement with his eyes fixed on the development of a *process,* was undoubtedly actually disappointed by the fact that the techniques on which he was working had only limited possibilities of destruction! The crisis typified in this published response is the source of a poignant feeling of impending confusion that is present in a statement of a preeminent physical scientist, J. Robert Oppenheimer.

Speaking of a "perpetual, precarious, impossible balance between the infinitely open and the intimate" and calling for it to be the "measure of our virtue that the limits of our powers correspond to some special wisdom in our choice of life, of learning or of beauty," he says, in words of evident pathos:

[8] Wolfgang Köhler, *The Place of Value in a World of Facts* (New York: Liveright Publishing Corporation, 1938), pp. 7–10.

[9] July 1950.

This is a world in which each of us, knowing his limitations, knowing the evils of superficiality and the terrors of fatigue, will have to cling to what is close to him, to what he knows, to what he can do, to his friends and his tradition and his love, lest he be dissolved in a universal confusion and know nothing and love nothing.[10]

We are becoming partial men, and it becomes more and more difficult to be whole human beings responding to the totality of life's potential. The fragmentation of modern man is both illustrated by, and helps to explain, what has happened in our era to art, music, and literature. They are all marked by the deliberate effort to break traditional structures. Coherence and harmony were foundation stones of aesthetic theory. Today, abstraction breaks up the world of color and relation, or spontaneity makes an assault upon discipline. The same rebellion in music produces atonality and dissonance. In literature, grace of style and the evocative power of the word are put aside for a new realism pointing up life's absurdities or for bold experiments in juxtaposition that scuttle meaning for mood-portrayals or abstract patterns.

Great art always expresses the mood of its day. The stylized and elongated forms of pre-Renaissance church art spoke of an other-worldly focus and a despair of finding abiding beauty in what the life of this world presents to us. In the fifteenth century, when the art and literature of classical antiquity began to emerge from the obscurity in which the Dark Ages had shrouded them and to open men's eyes to human potentiality, the way was paved for the superrealism of a Michelangelo with its joyous affirmation of the body and its message of the dignity and capacity of man. The same correspondence exists today. Fragmentation in the arts, abstractions and atonalities, tortured prose and incomprehensible poetry, powerfully and appropriately express the confusion, the groping, the hollowness, and the loss of direction of the middle of the twentieth century.

"Every work of art is the child of its time; often it is the

[10] J. Robert Oppenheimer, Closing Address, Bicentennial Celebration of Columbia University, New York, New York, December 26, 1954.

mother of our emotions," says Kandinsky, who was not only a great abstractionist but also a penetrating analyst of the art he helped bring into being. "It follows that each period of culture produces an art of its own which cannot be repeated." And then he adds: "Only just now awakening after years of materialism, our soul is infected with the despair born of unbelief, of lack of purpose and aim." [11]

Concomitant with this breakdown, we have been witnessing the dehumanization of man, which comes about, as Nicolas Berdyaev has trenchantly said,[12] when man is generalized and the individual human being no longer has value. This is evident in the mathematics of destruction in which the operators of electronic computing machines are able to deal "realistically" with our capacity to survive a nuclear attack in which 60,000,000 or more men, women, and children would meet their death in instantaneous annihilation or the slow agony of burns and poisoning.

The loss of a structure of meaning thus has a double effect: first, on society, in the increasing impermeability of barriers between group and group, nation and nation, power bloc and power bloc; second, on the individual, who, stripped of his value, is cut off more effectively than ever from his fellows.

Albert Einstein expressed concern about this problem in a lecture delivered at Princeton Theological Seminary:

> It is true that convictions can best be supported with experience and clear thinking . . . but those convictions which are necessary and determinant for our conduct cannot be found solely along this solid scientific way . . . The knowledge of what *is* does not open the door to what *should be* . . . to make clear these fundamental ends and valuations is the most important function of religion in the social life of man.

That institutional religion has so often failed to provide an authoritative and effective center of these fundamental ends and

---

[11] Wassily Kandinsky, *Concerning the Spiritual in Art* (New York: Mayflower, 1955; London: Vision, Publishers, 1955), pp. 23 f.

[12] Nicolas Berdyaev, *The Fate of Man in the Modern World* (Ann Arbor, Mich.: University of Michigan, 1961), p. 26. See also Chapter II, "Dehumanization."

valuations is one of the disappointing aspects of what is happening to modern man. The appropriate words are spoken on ceremonial occasions, and our political leaders in the West frequently give formal expression to religious sentiments. The words, however, no longer carry suasion or sanction. They are ornamentation for previously determined positions—not the dynamic determinants of the choices of men and nations.

Religious thought has been invaded by what has been called "the ethic of the possible"—a position that accepts as a necessity the modification of ethical imperatives in the light of the practical demands of the moment.[13] The statements of organized religious bodies frequently have this character. They say, "Yes—but . . ." rather than chance an absolute "No!" They are for peace *but* for the maintenance of our military strength. They are opposed to nuclear testing *except* as it may be necessary to that strength. Along with those of all other segments of society, their judgments are determined by the strategy of the power struggle and by the limitations of what is "politically possible," particularly with respect to the looming and all-important issue of our time: the threat of nuclear war.

It is true that the exaltation of expediency over principle is nothing new. Men and groups in the past have acted evilly and made immoral choices because they recommended themselves as practical. But they were under judgment. The prophetic spirit struggled against their sins. Guilt and repentance shaped recurrent rebellions so that the fallen society might begin again its progress toward justice and humanity. From the fable of Nineveh in the Book of Jonah to the tortured reassessment of the American Civil War, the possibility of turning and regeneration has burst forth again and again. As long as men had a conviction that there was a "will of God," they had a standard by which to re-establish their direction, and they frequently wrote that direction into the form and structure of the new society.

Our own generation rationalizes its immoral choices, calling evil good and good evil, ignoring Isaiah's stringent warning that

[13] See Ernest Lefever, *Ethics and United States Foreign Policy* (New York: Meridan Books, 1957), especially pp. 23–26 and p. 180.

justice must be laid to the line and righteousness to the plum-met.[14] Even if we survive thermonuclear holocaust—and there is little evidence in the present situation to support a belief that we shall—a generation may well come into being that will re-gard the humanitarian end products of Jewish and Christian morality as fuddy-duddy remainders of an age that had not ma-tured into an acceptance of the rational implications of its world view. Cold, precise computation will determine action, not in accord with a transcendent direction, but within the context of each situation and its pragmatic demands.

The joker in this trend is that judgments of value cannot be determined by computation, and, therefore, the essential choices can never be made by machines. One set of calculations will frequently veto another. For example, we have been able to devise new and effective methods of controlling insect pests, but our insecticides not only threaten the ecological balance that na-ture had provided, but jeopardize human health and even life.[15] We labor to uncover the secret of cancer and its cure even as we poison the atmosphere with cancer-producing agents. We applaud the caution and the conservatism of one physician as he strives to preserve one human life, but at the same time we resist warnings of the danger in the rise of the radioactive con-tent of milk. The preservation of power prevails as a supreme value over the preservation of life. This is the point at which the choice must be made, *before* the computing begins.

The trend toward the dehumanization of man exists, but it is not irreversible. Meaningful religion capable of shaping our lives and our society may be moribund, but its death is not in-evitable. Recognition of a danger should not mean yielding to it. We may note the probability of nuclear destruction, but we may not abandon our effort to survive.

The trend exists, but it is possible to halt it through the re-generation of necessary convictions about the ultimate nature of the universe—convictions that will not outrage our reason

[14] See Isaiah 5:18 ff.; 28:14–17.
[15] See Rachel L. Carson, *Silent Spring* (Boston: Houghton Mifflin, 1962).

or our knowledge but that will provide an anchorage for our values and infuse into them the force of absolutes.

For this is the point at which empirical naturalism with its consequent relativism fails us. If everything is process, there is no room for criteria independent of process by which process may be judged. Unless our values have ontological status, the ethical and human qualities that bring the possibilities of meaning and enrichment to life must dwindle away.

And *this is what is now happening to man.*

Technology has made possible new communication mass media of unprecedented comprehensiveness and effectiveness. As society is progressively homogenized, there is a consequent winding down in the content of its culture. The gradual disappearance of differences means the decline of that intercultural process in which values are generated or strengthened. Ethnic end products may have a quaint popular appeal and even become fashionable for a time—as in the Broadway successes of *Finian's Rainbow, Plain and Fancy,* and *Fiddler on the Roof*— but outside the theater the mills of conformity continue to grind, and "far-out" American jazz conquers in London and Rome, in Tel Aviv and Bangkok. The "other-directed" man exhibited to us by David Riesman,[16] constantly striving to keep in touch with his neighbors, is in the middle of a situation in which everyone is taking his values from everybody else, like the inhabitants of that fabled Irish village who made a living by taking in one another's washing. Says Riesman:

> Today the solid citizen has given way to the "solid sender," the "good Joe," not solid enough to risk offending anyone and afraid of disobeying the subtle and impermeable injunctions of the contemporary peer group to whom he looks for approval. He is a sender and receiver of messages in a network of personal ties which, unlike the personal ties of a folk society, neither warm nor protect him.[17]

[16] David Riesman, *The Lonely Crowd* (New Haven: Yale University Press, 1950), pp. 17 ff.

[17] David Riesman, "The Saving Remnants," in *Individualism Reconsidered* (Glencoe, Ill.: The Free Press, 1954), p. 112.

In this situation, he is unable to enter into meaningful relationships with his fellows. Others are patterns to be emulated or tools to be used. He is always "on," always "operating." Stripped of those distinctively human qualities that inhere in fulfilled relationships, he is no longer an antonomous individual realizing others as autonomous individuals, but the "hollow man," the statistic, the number in the ever-more dehumanized polis.

Not surprisingly, he frequently loses confidence in himself and in the meaningfulness of his own life. This is the state of mind called "anomie" by Émile Durkheim and "alienation" by existentialist thinkers—a sense of being unregulated and rootless, bereft of secure standards and of a secure place in life. At times during the last four decades, this malaise has been epidemic. "About a third of my patients," said Carl Jung, "are suffering from no clinically definable neurosis but from the senselessness and emptiness of their lives. It seems to me, however, that this can well be described as the general neurosis of our time." [18]

The same kind of diagnosis was made by Jung's estranged master, the founder of contemporary depth psychology himself, but with a despair-laden twist. "The moment one inquires about the sense or value of life, one is sick, since objectively neither of them has any existence," wrote Sigmund Freud. [19]

There is an unhappy irony in this statement, written in a period of pessimism and in anticipation of his own death. More than any thinker in history, Freud has led men to scrupulous self-examination. Yet, he seems to rule out as a form of illness that whole area within which man must grapple for meaning and for controlling purposes. If it is "health" to keep the treadmill moving without wondering whether or not one is going anywhere, then it would be preferable to choose "sickness"—the

[18] Carl Jung, *Modern Man in Search of a Soul* (New York: Harcourt, Brace & Company, Inc., 1933), p. 70.

[19] In a letter to Marie Bonaparte, dated August 13, 1937, found in Ernest Jones, *The Life and Work of Sigmund Freud* (New York: Basic Books, 1957), III, 465.

kind of sickness that afflicted Socrates, who affirmed that "the life which is unexamined is not worth living."

Men do want their lives to make sense. They are capable of extreme effort and endurance, of sacrifice and suffering, when they are motivated by purposes they deem valid. The heroic soldier, the martyr saint, or the mother scrubbing floors to send her son through school may all be clichés of fiction and cinema, but they represent recognizable aspects of human experience. Both clinical studies and common observation testify that there is a basic human need to know that one operates within a context of significance.

Indeed, there is a school of contemporary psychiatry that believes this need to be the primary human motivation. Its members dissent from the Freudian emphasis on a "will to pleasure" as well as from the Nietzschean idea developed by Alfred Adler that the "will to power" is central, and in their place they speak of a "will to meaning." When that will is frustrated, according to Victor E. Frankl, the result is that state of inner emptiness that is the major challenge to present-day psychiatry. Dr. Frankl says, "Man lives in three dimensions: the somatic, the mental, and the spiritual. The spiritual dimension cannot be ignored, for it is what makes us human. To be concerned about the meaning of life is not necessarily a sign of disease or of neurosis. . . . Spiritual agony may have very little connection with a disease of the psyche." [20]

When a context of meaning *does* exist, man can overcome what would otherwise be blighting and destructive external circumstance. The experience of the Jewish people testifies to this. I find it illustrated in a paradox associated with a Jewish folk phrase, *"Es iz shver tsu zein a yid,"* which means, "It's hard to be a Jew." When the East European Jew who lived wholly within the tradition and was certain of his role in life said this, he usually did so with an ironic twist in the midst of the joyous fulfillment of his Jewish obligations. It may have been after eating an especially delicious Sabbath morsel, or while relishing

[20] Victor E. Frankl, *The Doctor and the Soul* (New York: Alfred A. Knopf, 1962), pp. ix–x.

the peace of the booth during the Feast of Tabernacles. He would smack his lips and exuding signs of his deep satisfaction say, "Ay! It's hard to be a Jew." What he meant was: Insecurity is real, the possibilities of pogrom are real, the difficulty of making a living is real—but when all is said and done, being a Jew, following the customs of our people, responding to the will of God, is a glorious privilege, and it is *really* a delight to be a Jew. The descendants of that East European Jew live in relative security, have good incomes and comfortable homes, but when they say, "It's hard to be a Jew!" they mean it! An informed observer of this change would have to conclude that the sense of role that was natural and secure in the fathers has been attenuated or broken in the sons.

This viewpoint has been caricatured as meaning that the individual finds himself only by losing himself. But the one who finds security of purpose within a committed group or a dedicated social movement does not lose himself. On the contrary, he *locates* himself within a context, instead of being lost within an everywhere and nowhere. This is one of the ways in which what Erich Fromm calls the "existential dichotomy"—the point of conflict between individual goals and the recognition of mortality—may be overcome. Man needs a "frame of orientation and devotion." [21]

Without a sense of role, stripped of the conviction that one has an assigned part, however small, in the drama of life, men begin to know that malaise of alienation and rootlessness. If one's identity is not meaningful, if the significance of the self is diminished, if one loses the capacity to effect and maintain significant relationships, life becomes either "a nightmare or a nausea."

This is why the healthy individual resists the conclusion that he has no assignment or responsibility within a larger scheme. He seeks a context of significance that will assure him of the importance of his daily strivings. He protests against meaning-

[21] Erich Fromm, *Man for Himself* (New York: Rinehart & Company, Inc., 1947), pp. 40–48.

lessness and persists in the search for meaning even when it eludes him.

It is difficult to hold on to one's sense of significance within the whirl of contemporary life. All that we have said about the submergence of the individual man in the complexities of a fast-moving, necessarily organized society comes into focus now. The individual is lost in the mass. He does what is "in" or what is done by the mass when he plays. When he works, he is part of the mechanism or a factor in the organization—expendable and facing the threat that he may be eliminated by a machine capable of taking over his functions. If, as we have affirmed, the trend by which content and humanity are being squeezed out of life is not irreversible, then we must face up to our responsibility to labor to reverse it.

These concerns are not unrelated to the problems posed by the death-of-God theologians, for as we shall see, they have frequently adopted a terminology and an intellectual position that aid and support the depreciation of man's role. When one of them belittles the social gospel movement and the utopian visions of traditional religion, and another suggests that with "God's death" nothing is morally indefensible, they must bear responsibility for the potential effect of their iconoclasm on the human condition.

The overarching question of our time might be phrased in this fashion: "Shall we stubbornly resist those trends in our culture, our intellectual life and our society that threaten to strip man of his distinctiveness, to make of him a faceless component in the 'lonely crowd,' or shall we yield to the increasing organization of life as a necessary factor of its increasing complexity?"

Strangely enough, there are those who say we should yield, who characterize the disappearance of an emphasis on the prime value of the human individual not only as inevitable but also as promising and good! It is to them that we now turn our attention.

CHAPTER THREE

THOSE WHO WOULD YIELD

When hard-line technologists, cyberneticians, and high priests of computerdom become enamored of the fantastic possibilities flowing from man's continuing inventiveness or rejoice in the prospects of a micrometrically engineered society, to the point that the preservation of human values is overlooked, one is not at all surprised.

We have already alluded to the capacity of men to wear blinders and to concentrate their attention on process to the exclusion of all other factors. The experts of the Pentagon quite understandably may be totally absorbed in the specific military problems that are set for them; a tranportation engineer may be immersed in the task of getting the most from here to there in the quickest and easiest way and will, secondarily, deal with safety factors in terms of percentage of risk against percentage of advantage; the urban planner may be involved in the given and the possible, seeking to do what is economically advisable, moving masses with the least measure of friction.

The artist, the humanitarian, the visionary must be looked to for the intrusion of noneconomic, nonlogistical factors. We expect them to worry themselves about such things as compassion, concern for people, comfort, and beauty. They must somehow get that concern onto the drawing boards and into the blueprints. We even expect them to protest from time to time that human lives are not expendable factors, that more is involved than problems of logistics, more at stake than efficiency.

When, however, the assurance that man is the proper environment of the machine rather than vice versa, or that the depersonalization that accompanies spreading urbanization is not only a fact, nor even only an inevitable fact, but that it is not really so bad after all—when these assurances came from pundits in the humanities and professors of divinity, then it *is* occasion for raised eyebrows.

The counsel to embrace joyfully all that grows naturally out of scientific discoveries and their application in new techniques has been offered persuasively—or frighteningly—in two books we shall want to consider. One is a set of coldly realistic "notes" entitled *Yestermorrow,* by Kurt Marek, who under his pen name of C. W. Ceram is well known as a popular interpreter of archaeology and its discoveries. In it he takes a position "beyond optimism and pessimism" and considers from the viewpoint of Spengler's philosophy of history the position of man as he moves from yesterday toward tomorrow.[1] The other is a work quite otherwise motivated but linked with Marek's slim volume in a disturbing affinity of stance, the much discussed book called *The Secular City,* by Harvey Cox, professor of theology and culture at Harvard Divinity School.[2]

Their writings should occasion more than surprise. Some of us will wonder what it will be like when we are really going full speed ahead down the road to 1984 and where, with such defections, the braking effort can be successfully centered.

We are accustomed to dire predictions about man's future. None has ever been more powerful or persuasive than the grim certainties of Amos of Tekoa in the eighth century B.C.E. with his explosive warning of inevitable doom, the "day of the Lord," which, opposing the popular thought of his time, he painted as a day of darkness and destruction. But humanity is still here, struggling and falling, surviving catastrophe and evil, reaching out into the unknown "like the inchworm on the end of the stem." In our day, the threat of dehumanization has been vividly pictured by gifted novelists. It was George Orwell who set *1984*

[1] Kurt Marek, *Yestermorrow: Notes on Man's Progress* (New York: Alfred A. Knopf, 1961), p. 6.

[2] Harvey Cox, *The Secular City: Secularization and Urbanization in Theological Perspective* (New York: The Macmillan Company, 1965).

as the fictional time of a mechanized world in which all human values, all spontaneity and creativity will have disappeared under the dictatorship of "Big Brother." Aldous Huxley describes, in his *Brave New World,* how genetic control will produce specialized humanoids catalogued as alphas, betas, and gammas, skillfully manipulated by psychological conditioning and drugs. And John Hersey, in *The Child Buyer,* posits the frightening possibility that human beings may be converted into brainwashed, automatic computing machines.

For Kurt Marek, *all* such writers are "mene tekel Utopians." Like Belshazzar trembling at his banquet of wine, they have seen the handwriting on the wall: *"Mene, mene, tekel upharsin"* — and know that man has been "weighed in the balances and found wanting." [3] Their satires speak words of warning to mankind. Marek, putting into words what may well be the prevailing unconscious drive of our time, would have us believe that he embraces wholeheartedly the very same implications of our dynamic technology that chill us in the works of the "mene tekel Utopians." Huxley and the others, he tells us, are inhibited by the fact that they stand within the hothouse of the "high cultures" that are dying. Marek's own realism enables him to take a clear, unprejudiced look at "man's progress." He pictures his "brave new world" not satirically but with unblinking acceptance.

Man, he says, stands today at a point analogous to that at which he stood 5,000 years ago when the high cultures were coming to birth. The new tool of the written word, new techniques for agriculture and for societal organization, new outlooks and new modes of inquiry, all presaged a totally new form of life, a new dimension. We today are on the threshold of an era entirely different from that out of which we have come. "We open our eyes like prehistoric man, we see a world totally new and feel within ourselves the potentiality of enormous deeds." [4]

With the death of the "high cultures," we shall move quite naturally into the next phase of human evolution, but the human

---

[3] Daniel 5:24–28; Marek, p. 12.
[4] Marek, p. 21.

intellect will not be a simple development out of the intellect of today. It will be *transformed*.[5] Our children, who will have sensory experience of the space-time factors described by the new physics, will actually think in dimensions that are closed to us. Man will certainly no longer be the measure of things, for already our speeds and our calculations have exceeded all human measure. The transformed intellect of the future will adapt to the fact that man is the environment of the machine.[6] True, man will have to feed the machine. But our environment feeds us; without the world of animals and vegetation, we could not exist in our supposed central position today. The machine will be central tomorrow. Freed of the restraints that the religions of the "high cultures" have imposed, men will make free and uninhibited use of the techniques that scientific advance will provide to them. He offers as one example the possibilities afforded by artificial insemination guided by eugenic knowledge: Our descendants may well bring into being, by scientific breeding, a race of "happy imbeciles" who will serve the intellectual elite, performing all menial tasks and handling all routine operations, as completely contented as the cows that manufacture our milk.[7]

[5] Marek, p. 37.
[6] Marek, p. 55.
[7] Marek, p. 29 f. That Marek's position is not just an off-beat and singular phenomenon is demonstrated by the community of viewpoint found in the writings of Professor Jacques Ellul of the University of Bordeaux. See his *The Technological Society,* tr. John Wilkinson (New York: Knopf, 1964). Says Wilkinson: "Ellul's paper urged the thesis that modern technology is, or soon would be, completely autonomous, that it had its own imperatives, which could only with difficulty be reconciled with human values, and that it already was or soon would be out of effective human control. Men, argued Ellul, had become the slaves of their erstwhile servant. To use Nietzsche's terms, the necessary reassessment of value would signify that the means-ends relationship had been reversed by technology; that man was no longer *the* end-in-itself of religion and philosophy but had become the material sub-stratum of the industrial machinery; that is, the means by which the new social order is being realized." ("Technology and Human Values," pamphlet published by the Center for the Study of Democratic Institutions of the Fund for the Republic, Inc. [Santa Barbara, California, September 1966], p. 4).

Those of us who are not yet "freed" of Judaeo-Christian inhibitions will find this an appalling picture. The society it por-
trays will achieve its efficiency by a horrendous destruction of
what we have come to esteem as most precious: the free, individual human personality seeking to fulfill itself and, in our
dream of evolution, increasingly capable of finding that fulfillment. Eliminate the "restraints," and the manipulation of men
will know no limits. Breed happy imbeciles, and society may find
it equally economical or feasible to select living individuals for
lobotomies or for sterilization. When the computing machines
and technological skills become the determinants of values,
tenderness and respect for others will be obsolete. With the
efficiency and specialization and static quality of the ant heap,
the society of tomorrow would serve the needs of those who had
seized its controls.

There is a vast difference between the way in which Marek
faces the world of tomorrow and the way in which Cox faces the
secular city. Cox does not go all the way. He wants to yield
and yet not yield. He is willing to accept the "language" and
the "style" that the city may bring, but his obvious hope is that
there will be no disappearance of that which is most precious
about the human person. To this extent and despite his pre-
tended boldness, he is still living within what Marek would call
the "hothouse" of the older cultures. This results in a host of
paradoxes. The supermarket checker is necessarily faceless and
yet, "God meets us" in the relationship with "a client, a customer, a patient, a co-worker." [8] He says that "religion is, in
a sense, the neurosis of cultures" and that "secularization corre-
sponds to maturation" but that "releasing" men to maturity is
"the work of the God of Creation, Exodus, and Sinai. Calling
them to maturity is the task of the community of faith." [9] Where
Marek says that Christianity is dead, and Dietrich Bonhoeffer [10]
says that religion is dead, but not Christianity, Cox says that

[8] Cox, p. 261; cf. p. 41.

[9] Cox, pp. 153, 36.

[10] The writings of Bonhoeffer referred to by Cox are listed in his
footnote 2 on p. 13.

religion and metaphysics are dead, and even Christianity may
be dead, but not God, and not necessarily the Church. No, say
Hamilton and Altizer. God is dead and religion is dead, but not
Christianity.[11]

This is not parody. It is a straight-faced presentation of the
confusions we encounter when we read the "radical theologians."

It is not easy to know what Cox is getting at. Wide-ranging,
omnivorous in his reading, and ebullient, he is, therefore, not
immune to casual error; but he frequently gives forth brilliant
insights and is always jolting and stimulating. His dicta correspond sufficiently to those of Marek to couple them together as
heralds of a grim new world. Marek, like Cox, is concerned about
"language." He tells us that words such as "myth," "destiny,"
"soul," and "symbol" have turned "stone cold," [12] just as Cox
affirms that secularization means "the breaking of all supernatural myths and sacred symbols." [13] Marek also distinguishes between town and metropolis, between church bells as the "symbol" of the former, where the siren is its modern counterpart.[14]
Marek says, "Nietzsche was still at war with Christianity; now
that the balance sheet of Christianity has been drawn up, Nietzsche's passion seems out of place." [15] Cox sounds the same note:

> The anti-Christian zealot is something of an anachronism today,
> a fact which explains why Bertrand Russell's books often seem
> quaint rather than daring and why the antireligious propaganda
> of the Communists sometimes appears intent on dispelling belief
> in a "God out there" who has long since been laid to rest.[16]

Of course, when Cox speaks of the death of "religion," he
uses the word in a specialized and limited sense. It means—for
him—the worship of a transcendent God and the formalities
attendant upon it; it means institutions, fanaticism, and a closed

[11] William H. Hamilton and Thomas J. J. Altizer, *Radical Theology
and the Death of God* (Indianapolis: The Bobbs-Merrill Company, Inc.,
1966). See Chapter IV in this volume.
[12] Marek, p. 10.
[13] Cox, p. 2.
[14] Marek, p. 9.
[15] Marek, p. 74.
[16] Cox, p. 2.

world view. This latter bias is made clear in what he selects as signs that obituaries for religion—including his own—are perhaps "premature": he cites "the self-immolation of a Buddhist monk, the rise of fanatic sects such as Soka Gakkai in Japan, the appearance of the Black Muslims in America. . . ." [17] If we are being summoned to the interment of manifestations such as these, some of us will recite the funeral service without regret. When Cox also attacks the social innocuousness of much institutional religion and derides its purely ornamental role, we can stand shoulder to shoulder with him. We can agree, too, that we must ultimately find new ways in which to "speak of God." But secularization is tightly linked by Cox to urbanization, to the growth of technopolis, with its concomitant anonymity and frantic mobility. All this is part of what we must accept when he announces the terms in which we must "let go" and yield to the secular city. "Secularization rolls on," he warns us, and "we must learn to love it in its unremitting secularity." [18]

Because of his distinctive and specialized terminology (e.g., "secularization" is inevitable and therefore to be embraced; "secularism" presents the danger of a new closed system of thought and is therefore a menace to be resisted) it is not always easy to know what Cox is talking about. He seems to be saying that we can yield to urbanization and yet not sacrifice either values (as they concern relationship) or enrichment. He wants the "church" to function as the avant-garde of social change and as servant of the secular city but without "religion" which "is, in a sense, the neurosis of cultures." [19]

Cox does not seek to refute the accuracy of that descriptive aspect of modern social thinking that depicts contemporary man as increasingly depersonalized, "faceless," and "hollow." He simply parodies it and attacks this form of criticism as "cheapened and trite."

Contra Cox, the specter of being reduced to a number or statistic was real and threatening to those students of the Berkeley,

[17] Cox, p. 3.
[18] Cox, p. 4.
[19] Cox, p. 153.

University of California, revolt who paraded with derisory signs that said, "I am a human being. Do not fold, spindle, or mutilate!" The sense of the menace of machine civilization was made dramatically overt among them. "There is a time," said student rebel Mario Savio, "when the operation of the machine becomes so odious . . . that you can't take part . . . and you've got to put your bodies upon the gears, and upon the wheels, upon the levers, upon all the apparatus and you've got to make it stop." [20]

What Cox is seeking to do is to show that "anonymity and mobility" have a "positive side" and a "certain congruity with biblical faith." [21] "Positive" is, of course, a term that has significance only in relation to one's values. And Cox *admits* that "it is in the realm of values and ethics that the nurture of secularization becomes most ambiguous and problematical." [22]

If the human person is a supreme value, then Cox's "positive" may become a negative insofar as anonymity and mobility prevent his realization as person. As for "congruity with biblical faith," this may simply be in accord with Cox's *post hoc* interpretation of that faith. This is particularly evident in his imputation to the Sinai Covenant of a "deconsecration" or relativization of values. He makes a wholly erroneous distinction between the Sinai Covenant, which he exalts—it "frees us"—and the "Law," which he condemns—it "binds us." He makes the incredible statement, based on the prohibition of graven images, that "It was because they believed in Yahweh that, for the Jews, all human values and their representations were relativized." [23] This places the Covenant in opposition to the Law, which is again distinguished from Gospel, and Gospel means "that which frees us to decide for ourselves." [24] While this is an interesting tour de force, it is dependent upon an arbitrary or prejudiced

[20] On December 20, 1964, as quoted in *Those Who Make the Waves* (Berkeley: University Church Council, 1965), p. 31. These students felt that "religion" in its best sense was an ally in their struggle. See also pp. 5, 26 f., 38.
[21] Cox, p. 39.
[22] Cox, p. 36.
[23] Cox, p. 32.
[24] Cox, p. 46.

definition of terms—prejudiced in the sense of preserving the misunderstandings of nineteenth-century Christian Biblical scholarship.

"Law," as all should know by now, is usually a mistranslation of *"Torah,"* which means teachings or doctrine, and which includes *"Mitzvah"* (really, a host of *"mitzvot"*), which is the demand made upon us by the Divine *under the Covenant.* "Torah" is therefore the content of *"B'rit"* or covenant, and it is what the covenanting people undertook to live by and to preserve. "Mitzvah," which is in turn both the Divine demand and the human response to that demand ("For this *mitzvah* which *I enjoin upon thee* this day . . . is in thy heart and in thy mouth that *thou mayest do it.*") [25] is the instrument by which the total covenant obligation is fulfilled.

"Law," says Cox, smothers individual responsibility and choice. But "Law" is an obsolete, Protestant color-word standing for the rich interplay of *"Torah"* and *"mitzvah,"* which in the experience of the Biblical faith actually enhanced individual responsibility. ("I call heaven and earth to witness against you this day, that I have set before you life and death, the blessing and the curse; therefore choose life that you and your descendants may live . . .") [26] Under the Covenant, God demands that the Jew live by *Torah,* but it is man who must *choose* whether to perfom the *mitzvah* or not. Cox equates acceptance of the "Law" as tantamount to being "other-directed"—but there is a far greater difference, as Riesman and his associates pointed out, between "other-directed" and "tradition-directed" than there is between "tradition-directed" and "inner-directed."

The two major symbols of urbanization for Cox are the "switchboard" and the "cloverleaf." The switchboard stands for that multiplicity of interconnections that give the city dweller a practical anonymity. The cloverleaf is the image of his ceaseless activity, which Cox designates as his "mobility." Both symbols leave something to be desired in their descriptive power—even

[25] Deuteronomy 30:11–14.
[26] Deuteronomy 30:19.

making allowances for the inexactitude of all imagery. An actual switchboard allows for a multitude of *individual* connections and, through them, it is still possible to reach a specific person. Perhaps a computerized grid, the control of which is totally automated and freed of the interfering personal will of the dialing subscriber, would more fully represent the city's potential "anonymity"—literally, "namelessness."

Nor does the "cloverleaf" or the term "mobility" describe the actual situation of the mass of urbanized men. The cars on a cloverleaf are going somewhere. They are in process of *changing* their direction, but they do have a direction and a goal. City man shuttles from home to work to play to home, but he is not really "mobile"—any more than are the "mobile homes" that stand on concrete foundations in so-called trailer parks. The "jet set" is mobile—and rootless. The masses in the cities seldom set foot in a jet or even in a prop plane. They do not have the wherewithal to do so. Their symbol is the pendulum—from work to play to work to play—or the treadmill, whose constant motion goes nowhere.

Cox's paean to urban man's freedom of choice is also a bit flat. He offers as an example the putative fact that urban man in a city of a million is free to choose among fifty films, whereas village men may have at best a choice between two. If such a freedom did exist it would not be the result of, or necessarily correlated with, urban man's anonymity. The choosing man in a city of a million need not by definition be faceless. But the fact is that this vaunted freedom of choice is a mirage. To say that when he chooses one among the fifty he makes a conscious decision *not* to see the other forty-nine films is to ignore the power of advertising or the mechanism by which "other-directed" city man gravitates to that which is "in" for his set. It blinks the way in which city man is steered toward the vulgar, the flamboyant, toward that which is, by any enduring standard, the *less* valuable.

The true, fully developed, "faceless man" will not choose. The machine that swallows his perforated card will make the choice for him, even—the portents are visible—his choice of a mate.[27]

Cox also hymns the virtues of an unlisted telephone number—this, he says, may give city man the privacy necessary to his selection of those with whom he wishes to have relationships.

Apartment dwellers, he adds, may "choose *not* to 'know' their spatial neighbors in any intimate sense," so that they may have "more time and energy to cultivate the friends they themselves select." [28] All that this really means is that an individual who preserves a sense of individual personal values, if he has the means and sets up a set of efficient barricades against the complex openness of the urban environment, may be able to protect his prime right to make choices and to keep his home relatively uninvaded—he may *cut down* the measure of his anonymity and mobility; he may build an island in the city. Here Cox is really arguing *against* immersion in the secular city and revealing his lack of emancipation from Marek's "hothouse."

The logical extension of this position is to be found in Cox's rejection of Martin Buber's primary-word dichotomy, "I-Thou" and "I-It," and in his tentatively projected new intermediate category "I-You," in which people may operate together as a team, or render necessary services to one another, or be courteous in casual contacts. Is there a faint suggestion of snobbery here or a proposition that in the midst of all the faceless there may be an "elite" that will retain the enrichment of individualism? A softer version of Marek's "happy imbeciles"? Cox says:

> In most of his relationships he will be dealing with people he cannot afford to be interested in as individuals but must deal with in terms of the services they render to him and he to them. . . . Supermarket checkers or gas-meter readers who became enmeshed in the lives of the people they were serving would be a menace.[29]

This is nonsense—and dangerous, repellent nonsense at that.

[27] Computer matchmaking is already a "multimillion-dollar business," according to reporter Bob Rose (The Chicago News, Jan. 14, 1967).
[28] Cox, pp. 41, 45.
[29] Cox, p. 41.

There is nothing to prevent the custodian of an apartment house from having a friendly and interested monthly exchange with the gas company's representative—that is, as long as they survive; for the advance of technology will soon make both of them obsolete. The reader and I can bring to mind the faces and personalities—perhaps even some of the problems—of supermarket checkers and service-station attendants at the locations we frequent.

Surely, human contacts have always fallen into different categories: casual or customary or intimate. But even a casual contact can effect a moment of meeting in which I am present to the "thou" of the other. This is where Cox betrays his misunderstanding of Buber's central point. Buber does not say that all of our relationships are, or even should be, in the category of "I-Thou." The world's work could not be carried on if we failed to respond on that level of operation and manipulation which is "I-It." Even in the most intimate relationships, "I-It" prevails and must prevail most of the time.[30] We operate, we communicate deliberately and verbally, we persuade, we sell, we rationalize, we manipulate. Indeed, we must, even when we seek that *total attentiveness to the other* that is characteristic of the "I-Thou" moment. Such moments are vouchsafed to us "by grace" and they can occur between two strangers passing each

---

[30] "I-It" is not a pejorative term. It is a fact of experience. "The primary word *I-It* is not of evil . . ." unless "a man lets it have the mastery" and "the continually growing world of *It* overruns him and robs him of the reality of his own I. . . ." (Martin Buber, *I and Thou*, 2nd ed. [New York: Charles Scribner's Sons, 1958], p. 46.) Further, and in direct response to the kind of error made by Cox, Buber wrote in 1929:

The notion of modern man that this turning to the other is sentimental and does not correspond to the compression of life today is a grotesque error, just as his affirmation that turning to the other is impractical in the bustle of this life today is only the masked confession of his weakness of initiative when confronted with the state of the time. He lets it dictate to him what is possible or permissible, instead of stipulating, as an unruffled partner, what is to be stipulated to the state of *every* time, namely, what space and what form it is bound to concede to creaturely existence. (*Between Man and Man* [New York: The Macmillan Company, 1948], p. 22).

other in a crowd—even between a customer and a checker at a supermarket.[31]

As for Cox's "I-You" category, its defect is that it is really "I-It"—remembering that for Buber "I-It" is a fact of life. I do not *realize* another human being as *person* through mere courtesy or through "operating" with him in a team, or through intellectual acceptance that he is a person. When I use a thing gently, it is still a thing. If the supermarket checker can be, and probably will be, replaced by a machine, he has been reduced to a thing.

In response to this fact I have founded a new crusading organization. It has no dues, no constitution, no meetings—and, so far, I am the only member of it known to me. I call it the Society for the Maintenance of Personal Relationships. As a member I must try to break through the wall of mechanization and impersonality to a smile and even to a conversation. This means joshing a long-distance operator about an area-code number, or kibitzing with a "drive-in" bank teller, or the like.

I recently, for example, tried to have the charge on a long-distance call reversed to me after my caller had hung up. After some difficulty, I succeeded in reaching a supervisor who told me it was impossible to fulfill my request. Why not? "The charges have already gone through, sir."

"Do you mean," I said, "that they've automated that, too?"

"Yes, sir!"

"Well, watch out, dear. You're next!"

It was an appropriately grim attempt at humor. But it produced a chuckle, a response, and believe it or not, even a few sentences about the perils of automation.

It is probably a losing battle. It gets more and more difficult, especially on the new push-button telephones, to get into contact with a *person* in the apparatus, and the line of cars behind me at the "drive-in" sometimes gets impatient. But I am not yet ready to throw in the towel.

[31] Buber, *I and Thou,* pp. 11, 17. See especially his "Postscript," pp. 130 ff. A fuller discussion of Buber's thought appears in Chapter Ten of this book.

True, as Cox asserts, "urban anonymity need not be heartless." [32] Unless, however, there is serious, dedicated and continuing effort to counteract its potential heartlessness, it probably will be so. Recent incidents of "passing on the other side" help put the response of the Good Samaritan in a new light.

In Kew Gardens, New York City, a young woman was assaulted three successive times and finally killed as *thirty-eight people*—any one of whom could have picked up a telephone and called the police—heard her screams but did nothing.[33]

In Albany, New York, a young man, who had been under care in a mental hospital, stood on a twelfth-story ledge and teetered back and forth for two hours, not knowing whether to jump or to allow himself to be coaxed back inside. In this instance, silence was broken in that degradation of spirit when mob excitement is translated into jeering and catcalls. While the spotlights played upon the sick young man, a crowd of 4,000 watched on the street below. "Jump! What are you waiting for? Chicken? Are you yellow? Jump!" were the shouts that came from the crowd. "Five to one, he doesn't jump!" and some began taking bets. A well-dressed man expressed his fear of missing the show: "I hope he jumps on this side."

Callousness is not an invention of modern secular society. It was heartlessness that caused the frustration of the Tower of Babel and confounded the speech of men, the rabbis of the Midrash tell us. The myth of the tower, it must be added, reflected an ancient moral judgment about what was the greatest secular city of that day—the technologically advanced, ziggurated, and towered city of Nineveh with its 100,000 people and much cattle. For who were these people who came into the plain of Shinar to build the tower? They were not just a hodgepodge collection of people. They were led by Nimrod, the mighty hunter, who wanted to do more than "get himself a name": He wanted power. He wanted to establish himself as the dictator of

[32] Cox, p. 45.
[33] See A. M. Rosenthal, *Thirty-eight Witnesses* (New York: McGraw-Hill, 1964).

the entire world. He wanted to unseat God so that he might himself rule in God's stead.[34]

The tower which grew under his direction was—according to one ancient source—seventy miles high. The top was in what *we* call "outer space"! The scaffolding ran up on both sides, on one of which the workers went up and on the other of which they came down. As they worked, they would occasionally grow careless. They might drop a brick or let fall a tool. When this happened, the chiefs of the work would look, shake their heads and say, *"Oi lanu!* Woe is us! How can we replace that brick? How can we replace that tool?" But when a human being, one of the workers, would miss his footing and would fall to his death below, they would turn their heads away and go on casually with their work.[35] Men were "expendable." Bricks were in short supply. Tools were hard to come by. But men could be replaced as fast as they were killed.

The insight of the rabbinic tradition is clear: Exalt things and techniques and you despise life; despise life and you despise God. But the process works the other way as well: Despise and unseat God and you will come to exalt things, and exalting things, to despise life. One cannot dismiss the ominous reality of this chain by saying that "urban anonymity need not be heartless."

Nor can one speak of contemporary "mobility" without confronting the inherent dilemma first posed by Paul Valéry: the conflict between mobility and rootedness, the problem of how to be mobile and still retain one's roots. The major threat to man does not lie in his mobility, either his vertical social mobility or his horizontal spatial mobility. It lies in the possibility that increasing motion will fragmentize groups and uproot individuals. But it is possible to be mobile and to retain one's roots—to serve mankind and man's particular needs in Calcutta to-

---

34 Talmud. Tractate *Pesachim* 94b top. (Soncino translation, p. 504 f).

35 Genesis 11 and the rabbinic commentaries on it. These include *Pirke de Rabbi Eliezer*, trans. Gerald Friedlander (New York: Hermon Press, 1965), Chapter 24, p. 176. See also Louis Ginsberg, *The Legends of the Jews* (Philadelphia: Jewish Publication Society, 1909), I, 177 f.

day and Chicago tomorrow. It means that even as we move, we move within an ambience of friends and groups, purposes and values. It means—as Cox understands when he contrasts Yahweh to the Baalim—that even as we move we exalt time above space, purpose above structure, the needs of persons above technical achievement. The whole of Jewish historical experience testifies to the fact that mobility need not mean rootlessness or anomie. The Covenant and the Torah—purpose and values— are *portable*.

The menace, then, is not the "cloverleaf" that facilitates our going, but the treadmill on which we go nowhere; not the switchboard that facilitates communication and multiplies possible choices, but the automated grid that directs and limits the choices of individuals; not motion, but directionless motion, yielding to "natural" consequences of the progress of technology at the expense of human beings.

Where Cox confuses us is that ultimately he, too, affirms this. "The idea of the secular city," he says, "exemplifies maturation and responsibility . . . urbanization designates the fashioning of new patterns of human reciprocity." [36] These are terms that woo acceptance, but one reads Cox feeling that he has already conceded victory to the very forces that will make maturation, responsibility, and reciprocity themselves archaic and outmoded notions.

It is his exuberant acceptance of the *processes* that urbanization has set in motion, coupled with his willingness to dump "religion" or to proclaim that it, along with "metaphysics," is no longer viable, that generates the fear that he wants to throw out the baby with the bath. That neither the language of a "three-storied universe" nor the idea that God took human form and entered history at its midpoint, is acceptable to sophisticated modern man or relevant to his needs, is a response dictated by any objective look at our intellectual situation. That the forward march of technology and the development of new and unforeseen automated procedures are inevitabilities is obvious to any-

[36] Cox, p. 109.

one who realistically assesses our human situation. But that there are religious responses—as we shall define religion—that are existent in the world today and that are adequate to these situations is the burden of our argument and the center of our task in this exposition.

Cox is representative of the "radical theologians" only in his boldness and in his effort to break with old and limiting terminologies. He is still, however, able to say "God." It is to those who cannot say "God" that we now turn our attention.

CHAPTER FOUR

THOSE WHO CANNOT SAY "GOD"

God is not dead to everyone who is unable to say "God." There
are those who have placed the word and the subject outside
their "universe of discourse." Like Laplace in his celebrated
response to Napoleon, they "have no need for any such hypothesis." They are agnostics who do not know or have no need to
know, rather than atheists who deny. One must respect their
scrupulousness and admire the sense of security that enables
them to wear intellectual blinders and limit so effectively their
fields of concern.

Albert Einstein occasionally expressed that point of view.
Some twenty years ago, I sat in conversation with him in a small
group on the campus of Princeton University. We were discuss-
ing the nature of Jewish identity, and he had described for us
the twofold roots of his own Jewishness: First, he said, he
shared the Jewish fate and it was simple prudence to join hands
with his fellow Jews in meeting Jewish problems; and second,
he cherished deeply those Jewish values—he used the German
word, *"Werte"*—that had come down to him out of the Jewish
past. It was at this point that I ventured the question, "Where,
Dr. Einstein, do you find a place in your thought for God?" He
fixed his large, compassionate eyes upon me and responded with
great gentleness, "I have no need for that construct. I am content with the *'logisch'* simplicity of the universe." [1] At that point

[1] This viewpoint is expressed more fully and more formally in Einstein's little book *The World as I See It,* authorized English translation
by Alan Harris (New York: Philosophical Library, 1949), pp. 27 ff.;
cf. pp. 91 f.

I thought to myself that only an Einstein could look at the
vast, bewildering complexity of our universe and pronounce
himself content with its logical simplicity! But Einstein found
room in his thinking for something that he called "cosmic religion," and his interpretation of Judaism led him to believe that
in its this-worldly emphasis, Judaism more nearly approached
being this kind of religion than did any other faith.

This kind of "reinterpretation" has been commonly employed
by modern thinkers. John Dewey, for example, in his Terry
Lectures at Yale University, retained the word "God" to describe the process that relates the means that men employ to
the ends that they seek to achieve: "The *active* relationship between the actual and the ideal." [2] His disciple, Mordecai Kaplan,
applying Dewey's idea of "reconstruction" to Judaism, sees God
in terms of empirical naturalism as the process that aids men
in realizing their ideals. Recognizing that men may have a sense
of God's "felt presence," he speaks of God as "the power that
makes for regeneration" or "for the regeneration of human nature" or for the fulfillment of other ideal ends.[3] Kaplan accompanies a reverent "transnaturalism," as he now calls it, with an
effort to preserve those *mores* and aspects of traditional Jewish
practice that for him are the "civilization" in which these ideal
ends are defined. This led his opponents to jibe at him by saying
that before Mordecai Kaplan says that there is no God, he reverently covers his head with a skullcap—since no pious Jew will
utter God's name with uncovered head! Another quip characterizes the Reconstruction movement in Judaism by saying that
when Orthodox Jews pray, they address God as "Lord of the
Universe"; when conservative Jews pray, they say, "Our God
and God of our Fathers"; the Reform Jews say "Our Father
which art in Heaven"; and the "Reconstructionists" say "To
Whom it may concern!" Of course, like all jests, these are unfair

[2] John Dewey, *A Common Faith* (New Haven: Yale University
Press, 1934).
[3] Mordecai Kaplan, *The Meaning of God in Modern Jewish Religion*
(New York: Behrman, 1937).

despite their germs of recognizable truth. Unlike the radical theologians who seek a "new language and a new style," Kaplan has sought to preserve the language and style of Judaism while investing them with modern meaning.

The new radicals are saying something quite different. They would dispense with the word entirely or at least declare a moratorium on its use. What many of them are saying is that the word "God" has lost all content. It communicates nothing meaningful, and no propositional statement makes sense if it includes that word. This seems to be the position of a Michigan rabbi who, according to newspaper reports, is the first Jewish cleric to have excluded the word "God" from his congregation's worship services—if so anomalous a term may be used for his group's regular meetings. He calls himself an "ignostic" to convey his assertion that "when you say 'God,' I do not know [4] what you mean."

Edmund Wilson, the distinguished critic, is among those who have promulgated this view. In an essay on "Religion," he says that "The word *God* is now archaic, and it ought to be dropped by those who do not need it for moral support." Wilson continues:

> This word has the disadvantage of having meant already far too many things in too many ages of history and to too many kinds of people, along with the disadvantage that the one thing these various meanings have all had more or less in common is an anthropomorphic picture. In the case of the conceptions of the metaphysician—such as Whitehead's "principle of concretion" in the universe—in which the anthropomorphic image tends to disappear, this term seems far-fetched and uncalled-for; and in the case of the ordinary man, it is lazy to use it to designate the impetus which rouses him up from bed in the morning, sends him about his business and makes him believe that that business is important, as well as to provide a "first cause" that sets the ions of physics revolving around their nuclei and the planets around their suns.

[4] Presumably from the Latin *ignosco,* which really conveys the sense of "I overlook" or "I fail to notice." The rabbi referred to is Rabbi Sherwin Wine.

There is no classical conception of God that can really be made
to fit what we know today. . . .[5]

Certainly, when we use the word in order to talk *about* it,
rather than in the context of prayer or of poetic expression, we
should be conscious of the problems of communication. Of this
more will be said in the next chapter. But the problems of communication do not inhere only in the word "God." Every word
that has had a long history is emotionally charged and has meant
many things to many people. Even if we were to invent a new
word to express what the enlightened modern means when he
says "God," the new word would carry the freightage of the past.

But the "death-of-God" writers are not all of them talking
about language problems. Thomas Altizer and William Hamilton offer us ten possible meanings of "death of God," from "traditional atheism of the old-fashioned kind" to the recognition
that "our language about God is always inadequate and imperfect." [6] One group is saying that since this is a post-Christian,
indeed a post-religious era, all talk either about God or to God
is *de trop*—superfluous—and the whole idea is "culturally irrelevant." [7] A second group is protesting against hypocrisy
and desuetude in what goes by the name "religion," saying that
protestations about God have not been meaningful in the lives
of men, that religious institutions are not shaping or motivating
forces in contemporary society—they do not "count," and that,
therefore, God is, effectively and realistically speaking, absent.
A third group is simply giving expression to the view that there
is no God—or, at least, that no reality expressed by the word
"God" has ever been empirically demonstrated and so—they
say—we cannot assume that any such reality exists.

There is a fourth group of those who cannot say "God." It
is made up of those who in superficial and unsophisticated fash-

[5] Edmund Wilson, *A Piece of My Mind* (New York: Farrar, Straus
and Cudahy, 1956), pp. 6 f.

[6] William H. Hamilton and Thomas J. J. Altizer, *Radical Theology
and the Death of God* (Indianapolis: The Bobbs-Merrill Company, Inc.,
1966), pp. x f.

[7] For example, in Gabriel Vahanian, *Wait Without Idols* (New York:
George Braziller, 1964), p. 32.

ion associate the word "God" with primitivism and superstition and who themselves are beset with feelings of awkwardness in the presence of religious practices and religious ideas. These are matters that are not "modern." They are Sunday-school-level concerns—not for grown men in the twentieth century. They feel this inhibition most fully, I have noted, in the presence of their peers, apprehensive of what they may be labeled by their friends should they use seriously so old-fashioned a term as "God." It is not that they have lost faith in *man*. They are not those who, in the words of John Wilkinson, have learned to view themselves "as spontaneously generated bits of protoplasm, raddled with irrational fears and anxieties, and relegated to a rapidly shrinking rock in an absurdly out-of-the-way corner of the universe." Rather, they see themselves as makers and shakers who do not need the crutches and props required by the weaker souls who frequent churches and synagogues.

Obviously, the radical theologians are not in this class. They have viewed the whole range of Western intellectual development. They have inspected the latest defenses of traditional language forms and they have declared them, with expressions of deep agony, to be inadequate.

William Hamilton says:

> It used to be possible to say: we cannot know God but he has made himself known to us, and at that point analogies from the world of personal relations would enter the scene and help us. But somehow, the situation has deteriorated; as before, we cannot know, but now it seems he does not make himself known, even as enemy. This is more than the old protest against natural theology or metaphysics; more than the usual assurance that before the holy God all our language gets broken and diffracted into paradox. It is really that we do not know, do not adore, do not possess, do not believe in God . . . we take it as a statement about the nature of the world and we try to convince others. God is dead.[8]

Thomas Altizer considers both Paul Tillich and Rudolf Bultmann, the two pre-eminent influences in what was the most ad-

[8] Hamilton and Altizer, p. 27.

vanced Christian theology before the advent of the "death-of-God-radicals," and finds them both wanting. They either end in a "simple contradiction," he says, in that they would affirm both an immanent God who is the ground of our being and a transcendent God who is in "full continuity with the historic forms of the Christian faith" or they violate their own canons of theology by trying to harmonize a "partial immanence" with a "partial transcendence." [9]

This kind of logic is a final word only when positivist assumptions rigidly circumscribe thought and reject the possibility of the coexistence of contraries. Paradox, in which seemingly contradictory ideas are affirmed, is of the essence of religion and, indeed, may be of the essence of reality. Martin Buber makes this point in seminal fashion when he deals with the problem that is present in the great paradox of Rabbi Akiba: "Everything is foreseen and yet freedom [of choice] is given [to man]." [10] It is only, Buber says, in the world of strict logic that A and non-A cannot dwell together. In the world of life *as it is lived* we frequently experience *both* poles of a seeming contradiction as true.[11]

If this is difficult to understand, we have only to contemplate the fact that even our everyday physical experience in the modern world contradicts the previous rigid assumptions of common sense. As I write this particular paragraph, I am a passenger on a jet plane flying at 28,000 feet en route from San Francisco to Chicago. The pilot has just announced our position as a few miles south of Pierre, South Dakota. Get out your map with its classical Mercator projection and you will decide that we were either off course or flying the long way around—for, of course, in the strict canons of Euclidean geometry which, until the advent of Lobachevsky and others in what is really our own era, were regarded as incontrovertible axioms, "a straight line is the shortest distance between two points." But our pilot and the

9 Hamilton and Altizer, p. 11.

10 Talmud. Tractate *Avot* III:15.

11 Martin Buber, *Israel and the World* (New York: Schocken Books, 1948), p. 17.

authorities who govern aerial navigation have found a shorter way: the *curved* line, in this instance. As even we Euclid-bound old-timers must now recognize, the airplane following the curvature of the earth travels fewer miles than the railroad following the longer curve on the traditional Euclidean route that terrestrially limited surveyors have laid out.

My point is that just as our descriptions of the physical world are dependent on the perspective and the axioms from which we start, so in the world of ideas perspective is of controlling importance, and seeming contradictions may be resolved as the complex, multifaceted nature of the field under consideration becomes clearer.

This is what Buber suggests when he considers what happens when "reality is turned into logic" and "we get determinism and indeterminism, a doctrine of predestination and a doctrine of freedom, each excluding the other." He writes:

> The person who makes a decision knows that his deciding is no self-delusion; the person who has acted knows that he was and is in the hand of God. The unity of the contraries is the mystery at the innermost core of the dialogue.[12]

When we look forward and approach a choice, our consciousness of our freedom to go either way is unchallengeable. When we look backward after we have made our choice, the chain of causation seems to be complete. That there are thus two ways of looking at a matter—*l'chat'chila,* before it has happened, and *b'di-avad,* after it has happened—is a distinction preserved in Talmudic reasoning and jurisprudence. But an insistence on man's responsibility in making decisions is at the heart of Judaic thought: "I have set before you life and death, the blessing and the curse; Therefore, choose life." [13]

To say, therefore, that a sense of God's immanence must contradict a sense of God's transcendence is to turn one's back on the lush complexities and potentialities of all-that-is. The rabbinic interpretations of Scripture often demonstrate an aware-

[12] Buber, p. 17.
[13] Deuteronomy, 30:19.

ness of these characteristics of reality in their replies to the
logic-choppers and skeptics of the Greco-Roman world. One
such challenged a rabbi with the contradiction between Exodus
40:34 (". . . and the glory of the Lord filled the tabernacle")
and I Kings 8:27 ("Behold, heaven and the heaven of heavens
cannot contain Thee"). The rabbi affirmed both immanence and
transcendence by using as an analogy the picture of a cave by
the shore of the sea that the sea may fill without any perceptible
diminution of itself.[14] The rabbi's argument is admittedly not
precise—but this is an area in which, as we shall see in the next
chapter, precision tools destroy truth.

This kind of discussion is, however, itself outside the frame
of reference of the radical theologians. For the most part, they
do not feel obligated to offer a critique of the traditional theologies. The traditional theologies are "dead" as religion and metaphysics are "dead." Cox approaches his subject with the tools
of sociology, Paul van Buren uses the method of linguistic analysis, and Gabriel Vahanian makes his contribution through the
disciplines of literary criticism and culture analysis.

Because he is dissecting a "cultural concept" rather than
searching out a reality, Vahanian is able to say that it is "not
sacrilegious to speak . . . of God as the chief failure of man."
God is dead, he says, because concepts are valid only "so long
as they spearhead the spontaneous expression of a particular
human experience, they can live only as long as their cultural
framework lasts." [15]

For Vahanian, God is dead in the innocuousness of institutional religion, in what he delights to call "religiosity"—the stuff
and the trappings of religion. "The recent revival of religion . . .
has no other allegiance than to its own inauthenticity." [16] It is
inauthentic because it substitutes "togetherness," which is ro-
mantic and counterfeit, for genuine communion and genuine

[14] *Pesikta d'Rav Kahana*, 2b (Buber ed.), quoted by Solomon Schechter, *Some Aspects of Rabbinic Theology* (New York: The Macmillan
Company, 1909), p. 29 f. The entire chapter in Schechter, "God and
the World," will repay study.

[15] *Wait Without Idols*, p. 229.

[16] Gabriel Vahanian, *The Death of God* (New York: George Braziller, 1961), pp. 5, 192–193.

faith. It is the American faith in faith, which asks of religion only "peace of mind" or assurance of material success.

In this form, the death-of-God pronouncement seems to be but the sensational slogan of a salutary social criticism. The emptiness, the inauthenticity, the shoddiness of so much that is called "religion" requires excoriation and rejection. Vahanian does not seek to evade the implications of this approach. "From this point of view," he says, "the death of God may be only a cultural phenomenon as though only our religio-cultural notion of God is dead." [17] But the pronouncement obviously means more than that—we must view it in terms of our legacy from both Kierkegaard and Nietzsche.

> To say that God is dead [as did Nietzsche] or to assert an infinite qualitative difference between God and man [as did Kierkegaard] means not only that no ladder leads from man to God; it also means that there is no identity of substance between man and God, and, accordingly, that the problem of human existence is independent of the problem of God.[18]

Pursuing his culture analysis, Vahanian distinguishes between "secularity" and "secularism." "Secularity" is equivalent to the Biblical emphasis upon our obligations in this world, and as such it is the "realm in which religion can show its relevance," whereas "secularism" is a "form of religiosity in which the present and the immanent are invested with attributes of the eternal and the transcendent." The Social Gospel, as represented by Josiah Strong and Walter Rauschenbusch, at the turn of the century, prepared the way with its meliorism and Pollyannaish optimism, says Vahanian, for the coming of secularism.[19]

In this, Vahanian neglects the rigor, the cry of protest, and the penetrating social criticism of the Social Gospel movement. As a Judaizing heresy, it was posessed of an awesome sense of God's demand. It was not only a faith in the establishment of God's kingdom upon earth, it was an insistent emphasis on

[17] *The Death of God*, p. 231.
[18] *The Death of God*, p. 210.
[19] *The Death of God*, pp. 60 ff., 67, 28 ff.

"what the Lord doth require." If it prepared the way for the coming of "secularism" it was only through the degeneration and ultimate subversion of its message.

Josiah Strong, says Vahanian—evidently to deprecate the significance of the Social Gospel or deny it meaning as "religion" by calling it the precursor of "religiosity"—was in favor of institutional churches "which he considered thoroughly prepared and equipped to tackle the multitude of social and economic problems created by the exodus from the country to the city." [20]

But this is a role currently being played by the most dynamic and most alive religious institutions, least susceptible to denigration by the word "religiosity." Consider Father John Shocklee in his St. Bridget of Erin parish in St. Louis, seeking in 1966 to "break through the walls of the sanctuary" and in response to God's demand carrying his ministry, in a wide range of creative projects, to the most impoverished of his community; the Beneficiary Congregational Church in Providence, Rhode Island, building open-occupancy low-income housing in the central city; synagogues engaged in Job Opportunity programs and in mobilizing volunteers for tutorial work, for Head Start programs, and for receptivity in changing neighborhoods— in response to the Jewish ideal of *kiddush ha-chaim,* making God's presence manifest in life. All of them may be the most effective harbingers of the new tidings that God lives, rather than forlorn and reluctant witnesses of God's death.

Vahanian seems to fear that the ideals of the Kingdom were in danger of being realized and that "Christianity was perishing of its own realization." [21] Those who hear the address of God's demand upon society today have no "fear" that the Kingdom is at hand. They know that, laboriously and with constant recognition of both the Source and the Goal, they must build it.

It is in his characterization of our era that Vahanian is at one with Harvey Cox. The culture of our times is "post-Christian" in that the world has been "deprived of sacramental significance." Essentially, he is penning a protest against man's "mur-

[20] *The Death of God,* p. 31.
[21] *The Death of God,* p. 36.

der" of God and against the horizontal dullness of a world that has been stripped of its capacity to reach out toward commanding values and toward the inner enrichment of the lives of men. His cry is: ". . . if we can no longer assume that God is, we may once again realize that he *must* be." [22]

Another of the new "radicals" is torn by no such yearning for the God who "must be." For Paul van Buren, God is wholly dead: he is unable to say "God" at all. His major concern is to save Christianity—obviously a Christianity without God. In this, he follows Dietrich Bonhoeffer, whose courage in facing the theological problems of what he called "a world come of age" matched the heroism with which he gave his life in resisting the thought control of the Hitler government. Van Buren is seeking to find an appropriate way for a Christian in such a world "to confess his faith in Jesus Christ." [23] This is the core of the effort that Bonhoeffer made and that van Buren sees himself carrying forward—a specifically Christian effort in a particularistic Christian problem.

Bonhoeffer, however, never proclaimed the "death of God." He adopted an "as if"—a necessary fiction that did not deny the reality it blocked off. He said, "Honesty demands that we recognize that we must live in the world as if there were no God. . . . We stand continually in the presence of the God who makes us live in the world without the God-hypothesis." [24]

For Bonhoeffer, this paradox is the heart of the dilemma. Van Buren cuts it away with the surgical tool of contemporary "linguistic analysis." He is constrained to accept the "empirical way of thinking and of seeing the world" that the scientific revolution has given us, and he offers as his stance ". . . a deep interest in questions of human life this side of the 'beyond' and

---

[22] *Wait Without Idols*, pp. 31, 33, 46; cf. p. 223.

[23] Paul M. van Buren, *The Secular Meaning of the Gospel* (New York: The Macmillan Company, 1963), p. 2.

[24] Quoted (p. 1) in van Buren from Dietrich Bonhoeffer, *Widerstand und Ergebung* (Munich, 1951), p. 241. The American edition is *Prisoner for God* (New York: The Macmillan Company, 1959); the English edition is *Letters and Papers from Prison* (London: SCM Press, 1953), pp. 163 ff.

a corresponding lack of interest in what were once felt to be the great metaphysical questions." [25]

From this position, van Buren maintains that "modern man," whom he defines as all those who stand within his own definition of the "empirical way of thinking" is unable to speak of God even in metaphorical or poetic concepts. He tells us that to anyone "who shares the empirical spirit of our age" oblique language about God is no more useful than "objectifying" language. "The problem," he says, "lies in the word 'God' itself, and in any other word supposedly referring to the 'transcendent.' " [26]

Here arises the problem of preserving Christianity without "God-language," and the problem is complicated by the fact that there can be no Christianity without the Christ. Van Buren has set for himself an intricate problem, the solution of which will require the greatest ingenuity. He does not quite bring it off, despite a brilliant tour de force, in the frame of reference he has chosen. The alternatives for *Christian* secular man, says van Buren, are to "forget about the Gospel and abandon his Faith" or to find "a secular way in which to understand it." [27] Since van Buren, for reasons that he does not give, does not want him to do the former, he must erect a structure that will help him do the latter—which means to understand the Gospel in terms of his life in this world.

The peculiarly Christian problem, which non-Christians may view from the outside without a sense of identification, inheres in the role that belief or affirmation plays—indeed, must play— in Christianity. Without the assignment of a special role to Jesus as the Christ, there is no Christianity. The new Christian theology is especially fond of the old Greek word *kerygma,* and *kerygma* is the apostolic proclamation that "Jesus is Lord," the proclamation, when the tomb was found to be empty, that Jesus had risen. Without the *kerygma* there is no Christianity: van Buren himself says this, echoing Bultmann: ". . . the

[25] Van Buren, pp. xiv, 5; cf. p. 17.
[26] Van Buren, p. 68.
[27] Van Buren, p. 78.

kerygma alone offers man the possibility of this new existence, and the *kerygma* is grounded in the event of Christ." [28]

It is this central need that makes theology so important in Christianity, and it is the possibility of "salvation" as defined in the primal meaning of this event that has turned normative Christianity through the ages to the "beyond." Having defined "religion," as Bultmann did, as "the human longing to escape from this world, fed by the supposed discovery of 'a sphere above this world, in which the soul alone, released from all that is worldly, could repose,' " [29] or, as Bonhoeffer did, as "the attempted 'enlargement of reality by means of God' " which means metaphysical or other-worldly thinking,[30] the radicals must then seek to dispose of religion as dead, or seek new "nonreligious" interpretations of traditional concepts.

This problem does not beset a religion whose primary concern is this world and man's responsibilities in it, which sees God not as a means of enlarging reality or explaining it but rather as the Source of *mitzvah,* of the Demand made upon man that he perfect the world until in its respect for life it reflects God's Kingship.

But for van Buren, theology is Christology, and if he must give up the Father, he chooses to hold fast to the Son.[31] Christianity is a "historical faith" and that "history," which he defines in *empirical* terms rather than as salvationist history (*Heilsgeschichte*), has to do "with a particular man who lived and died in Palestine." [32] An historical event may produce a "discernment situation," but it cannot do so, says van Buren, unless the event has actually occurred. This creates problems, for the material we have about Jesus was "not intended to be documentary evidence of historical or biographical 'facts.' It was a story in the service of the Easter *kerygma*." Nevertheless, van

28 Van Buren, p. 6; cf. p. 59.
29 Van Buren, p. 81, quoting from Rudolf Bultmann, *Kerygma und Mythos,* ed. H. Bartsch (Hamburg: Herbert Reich-Evangelischer Verlag, 1948), I, 26 f.
30 Van Buren, p. 82.
31 Van Buren, p. 42; cf. p. 79.
32 Van Buren, pp. 109 ff.

Buren insists on the importance of the historical event: "Faith is not based simply on a picture of the historical Jesus, but the historical Jesus is indispensable for Faith." [33]

Thus, van Buren must search for the historical core of meaning in the life of "a man who actually lived, died, and was buried." He must historically define the way of life that Jesus followed and relate it to the "Easter discernment situation" out of which there "arose a commitment to the way of life which Jesus had followed." [34]

He finds this in his extraction from the Gospels of a picture of Jesus as a "remarkably free man," one who was "free to be compassionate for his neighbor, whoever that neighbor might be, without regard to himself," and whose freedom became "contagious" in the Easter event. This must, in the context of his objective, be a unique freedom, empirically distinguishable from the freedom of Socrates, which might nonetheless have a liberating effect on all Socratics, as the freedom of Jesus has a liberating effect on all Christians.[35]

In saying this, van Buren has said too little from the standpoint of believing Christians and too much from the standpoint of empiricism. For even this modicum of affirmation about Christianity's central and necessary figure cannot be verified according to the strict canons of empiricism. From van Buren's own "scientific" point of view, the affirmations he makes would have to be regarded as affirmations about events of doubtful and undemonstrated historicity or about a received image of those events that distorts the little historical evidence we possess.[36]

Central to his defense of his last bastion of what can be called Christian is his statement that the Easter event was a crisis experience, a "discernment situation" for the disciples out of which "arose a commitment to the way of life which Jesus had fol-

---

[33] Van Buren, pp. 118, 126.
[34] Van Buren, pp. 132 f.
[35] Van Buren, pp. 121, 123, 132 f.
[36] Van Buren's effort in accordance with his painful task is to be scrupulously honest about this (see pp. 9 ff. and p. 54).

lowed." Ignoring the wrathfulness, the unkindliness, and harshness in the Gospel picture of Jesus (as in Matthew 23) and positing for the sake of van Buren's argument a way of life that was exemplary, it cannot be said, without ignoring a large body of received knowledge, that the Easter event produced among the disciples a commitment to his way of life. What the Easter event may be said to have produced was a commitment to the idea that since Jesus had risen he was proven to have been the Messiah and he was therefore "of God." Christological event produced a theological affirmation. As for the commitment to Jesus' way of life, it can more easily be said in accordance with the received facts of the followers of Jesus that they were frequently martyrs but they were only rarely "remarkably free" and "compassionate."

The dilemma is made clear when we read the twenty-fifth chapter of Matthew. If it depicts the historical Jesus, then the historical Jesus can hardly be described as "compassionate." If it describes the disciples' view of Jesus or even the view of the Evangelists, then the *kerygma* cannot be described as having produced a commitment to Jesus' way of life. For in Matthew 25 is the parable of the sheep and the goats. In it, Jesus is depicted as proclaiming that the "worthless servant" will be sent into "outer darkness" where "men will weep and gnash their teeth." And "when the Son of Man comes in his glory," he will separate the sheep from the goats, and the sheep will be on his right hand and the goats will be on his left hand. Then he will say to those at his left hand, the "goats," those who have not accepted his divinity and, thus, more than half of mankind: "Depart from me, you cursed, into the eternal fire prepared for the devil and his angels; for I was hungry and you gave me no food, I was thirsty and you gave me no drink, . . . as you did it not to one of the least of these you did it not to me." And "they will go away into eternal punishment," into damnation, hell-fire. This is not "compassion."

The fact is that it is almost impossible to view Jesus meaningfully in van Buren's frame of reference as a historical figure and a human being. Jesus *is* a historical figure, but viewed by

Christian tradition, Jesus was God incarnated in sinful, human form. And if Jesus was God incarnated as sinful, contingent, and imperfect man, his *human* failings do not matter. This was the purpose of God's having become flesh: to take on the *sins* of mankind. Thus, in the traditional view, the imperfections of Jesus as man square with the view of Jesus as divinity.

The alternative view of Jesus presents difficulties. If Jesus is to be exalted and admired as an exemplary human being, then we are forced to substitute a haze of selected images for the details presented to us in the Gospel story.

In viewing the Easter event as the crucial discernment situation, van Buren is not concerned with explaining the empty tomb, and he is certainly not concerned with defending a "resurrection" with its theological significance. His main concern is with its psychological significance, with what it meant to the assembled disciples and what it means to those who receive it. But if only the empirically demonstrable is "real"—and for most of the radicals the *kerygma* is not immune to the demand for demythologizing [37]—then the problem cannot be solved by van Buren's linguistic analysis.

Either we must view van Buren's effort as a specialized theory that grows out of two arbitrary a priori statements: One, that the centrality of Jesus as the Christ is beyond cavil; and, two, that the Christ is redefined in a new and humanistic view of the *kerygma*—or, we must accuse him of a "misleading use of words" with respect to such words as "Lord and Saviour" and "Christian faith" even as he is busy avoiding the word "God" for fear that it will be misleading.[38] In either case, he is hoist by his own petard. If it is a specialized theory comparable to those specialized geometries that are founded upon arbitrary axioms, it is not "empirical" in the usual sense, nor would it be readily acceptable to one who, in van Buren's own terms, "shares the empirical spirit of our age." If it is simply a carelessness in the use of terms that have acquired deeply changed meanings in the course of two millennia of Christian history,

---

[37] See Hamilton and Altizer, p. 10.
[38] Van Buren, p. 145.

then he is guilty of that "mixing of language-games" of which he accuses others.[39]

One suspects that the difficulty that besets van Buren and others and makes it difficult for them to say "God" is not the difficulty imposed by too great a measure of scrupulousness in the use of language. Rather it grows out of a view of language that is far too limited and circumscribed and that neglects the richness of the varied roles of language by reducing all speech and argumentation to the level of "language-games." It is an approach that inadequately apprehends the mystery of language, even as the unwary profaner of its shrine is himself captured by its drama.

Words—especially the word "God"—are dynamic and alive. They do not meekly lie down for analysis. For words live through the succession of changed situations that make up the history of the men who use them. The word "God," like other words, is apprehended differently by the successive generations of those who seek to express their consciousness of God's presence and God's demand. Judaism gives voice to this insight by speaking of "the God of Abraham, the God of Isaac, and the God of Jacob." [40] The repetition of the word "God" three times has, we are told, more than ordinary significance. Indeed, that repetition is intended to alert us to the fact that God was differently understood, His presence differently manifested, and His relationship differently perceived by each of the three patriarchs and, hence, it may be inferred, by all the succeeding generations. The "Malbim" (Meir Löw ben Yechiel Michael)—one of the pre-eminent nineteenth-century Bible commentators—says the verse means that the names by which God is called, and in which His special providence is made manifest, and the manner in which His presence abides in the midst of those who relate themselves to Him—all this "changes in every generation ac-

[39] Van Buren, p. 64.

[40] Exodus 3:15, and the first paragraph of the major prayer sequence of Jewish worship. For example, see *The Authorized Daily Prayer Book,* ed. Joseph H. Hertz (New York: Bloch Publishing Company, 1959), p. 131.

cording to their deeds and their worthiness . . . in other words, that manifestation of divinity (*ha-elahut*) that rested on Abraham was a manifestation different from the one that rested on Isaac, and in a different category from that which occurred to Jacob. . . ." [41]

This protean character of the most revered of words does not entitle us to dispense with its use. We cannot avoid saying "God." Were we to follow Edmund Wilson's advice and discard the word as "archaic," what vocable would take its place? What word would we substitute for it to express our apprehension of the Whole, of ultimate significance, and of ultimate demand? What would be the vocable we would use to stand for the other pole in our relationship to all-that-is?

Martin Buber is right: we must respect the word and recognize that all who use it and all who have used it, however haltingly and by whatever name and in whatever language, have always had one ultimate reality in mind. That reality is the source of relationship and the source of significance.

We must redeem the word so that it will express all that the modern religionist feels when he turns away from mechanization, from fragmentization, from trivialization, and when he turns *toward* the source of value and the source of morality. The word "God" is necessary to us, not for ritualistic or formal use. The word is necessary because of the reality that it evokes when we become conscious of the demand that we deal reverently with life, because again and again in our life-situations, we find that no other word will do.

When we submit our aspirations to the highest judgment, we say "God." When we address the world and respond to it in awe and amazement, in gratitude and in humility, we say "God." When we fill with tears as we confront manifestations of sensitivity, of compassion, and of human achievement, we say "God." When we behold unselfishness in action, sacrificial courage in behalf of human dignity, concern for justice, loyalty and perseverance, we say "God." When we catch a glimpse of truth, not

[41] Malbim, *Hatorah V'Hamitzvot*, "Commentary on Exodus" (New York: Grossman's Publishing House, 1964), p. 27.

the truth of one-plus-one but the abiding verities that lift a corner of the curtain to assure us that there is *indeed* meaning, we say "God." When we strive to place our own small lives within the context of a grand design, we say "God." When we say the word, to which there clings the aura of the ineffable, we say it reverently. We know that we hear "but the whisper of His ways," but we say it as our fathers through the ages have said it.

We say "God"—and when we step back for analysis we know that "God" is a word. The fact that it *is* a word does not *reduce* its significance. On the contrary, it enhances its content and enriches its mystery. How it does so is the subject to which we now turn our attention.

PART TWO

ELEMENTS OF DEFENSE

Para pensar cual tú, sólo es preciso no tener nada mas que inteligencia.
Unamuno

In order to think the way you do, it is only necessary to have nothing more than intelligence.

CHAPTER FIVE

"GOD" IS ALSO A WORD

The word "God," we are told, is a vocable of doubtful utility. It has been charged with so many layers of meaning, it has been so abused and misused, that it fails to communicate any meaning at all.

This judgment is, as we have seen, one of the factors that motivate those who cannot say "God." That they are not always quite so rigorous in their use of other terms and constructs is an indication that something more than a concern for semantic exactitude is shaping their conclusion in this matter. They are, as we have seen, willing to apotheosize Man, an idealized construct compounded of potentialities and hopes. Or, as with some of the Protestant radical "nontheologians," they would hold on to the Christ, a received concept built out of selected historical conjectures and certain aspects of the traditional image.

For some who have dispensed with the term "God," the added factor is the general malaise of our time, which leads many intellectuals to feel uneasy, indeed, "silly," [1] when they deal with matters associated in their minds with "supernaturalism," magic, or superstition.

This inhibition is not the result only of progress in studies of semantics and of language analysis, but it seems to be one of the accompaniments of civilization—one that has an increasingly important function as life grows more complex. Indeed, exactitude of communication is essential in science and technology. Martin Buber has pointed out that primitive languages are naturally and colorfully poetic and exhibit a naive capacity

[1] See below, Chapter Six, pp. 97–98.

for metaphor—contrary to our popular belief that the more primitive a language is, the simpler it is, and the closer to grunts, cries, and purrs. He cites the Zulu word for "far away," which is a single multisyllabic word that literally means, "There, where someone cries out: 'O mother, I am lost.' " [2]

We cannot return to the simple wonder and response of primitive man and we should not idealize his situation—it was frequently brutish and inordinately difficult. It must be apparent, however, and not only by a *reductio ad absurdum,* that were the process by which our use of language has grown increasingly exact and self-conscious to go forward to its logical end point, something precious would be stripped away from human experience. We would be learning to express ourselves in bare and aseptic mathematical formulas or in the signs and exponents invented by general semantics. [3]

More important, we would lose touch with aspects of reality, perhaps the most significant aspects, which can be dealt with meaningfully only in what Philip Wheelwright has called "soft focus." [4] Those who would reduce speech to the expression of what is empirically demonstrable would, were they successful, exclude from all possibility of expression a huge slice of human experience.

Indeed, rigid application of the principle of empirical verification would make it impossible for us to use any unqualified, ordinary language whatsoever. We could not say "God," to be sure. Neither could we say "Man." We could not even say "writing table." We should have to say "writing table in the small study to the right of the main entrance, 17626 Lomond Blvd., September 17, 1966, 11:01 P.M." Nothing less would

[2] Martin Buber, *I and Thou,* 2nd ed. (New York: Charles Scribner's Sons, 1958), p. 18. Compare Susanne K. Langer, *Philosophy in a New Key: A Study in the Symbolism of Reason, Rite, and Art* (Cambridge, Mass.: Harvard University Press, 1942), p. 142.

[3] For example, see Alfred H. Korzybski, *Science and Sanity: An Introduction to Non-Aristotelian Systems and General Semantics,* 3rd ed., rev. (Lakeville, Conn.: The International Non-Aristotelian Library, 1948), p. 428.

[4] Philip Wheelwright, *The Burning Fountain* (Bloomington: Indiana University Press, 1959), pp. 62 ff.

communicate exactly. The important point, however, is that even this form of semantic would be inadequate to certain aspects of experience: the sublimity of a sunset, the sense of exaltation generated in a particular symphonic passage, the insight that love is better than hate. Nor is any one of these empirically verifiable in the sense in which we seek verification of a scientific hypothesis. They are insights and responses that fall into the realm of evaluation rather than description, of expression rather than designation, and are not susceptible to empirical test. And just here is the stumbling block in the path of those who seek to ground value theory in empiricism. It may be that long-range experience will "validate" certain values, but values cannot be subjected to "verification" without the creation of an arbitrary principle of verification.[5]

This is the problem confronted by Paul van Buren when, as we saw in the preceding chapter, he attempts to make the insights and the value responses of a rich tradition conform to a specific verification principle.

His starting point, as a Christian theologian searching for a new language and a new style, is nonetheless necessarily within that tradition, and he speaks out of his commitment to it. He is using "language analysis" not for itself but as an instrument for an ulterior purpose—to "save" Christianity. Bishop Robinson is far more daring in stating his central bias and the nature of this kind of rescue mission, when he says, "Christianity stands or falls by revelation, by Christ, as the disclosure of the final truth . . . about all nature and all reality." [6]

Because van Buren has dispensed with the word "God" as being beyond the reach of his "verification principle" and because—as we have seen—he wishes to retain the person of Jesus and the importance of the Easter proclamation as presented in the Gospels, he is forced to deal with the fact that the person,

[5] See Henry Margenau, "The Scientific Basis of Value Theory," in *New Knowledge in Human Values,* ed. Abraham H. Maslow (New York: Harper & Brothers, 1959), pp. 48 ff. See also Paul Tillich, "Is a Science of Human Values Possible?" pp. 189 ff. in the same volume.

[6] John A. T. Robinson, Bishop of Woolwich, *Honest to God* (London: SCM Press, 1963; Philadelphia: The Westminster Press, n.d.), p. 128.

Jesus himself, stood in a relationship to God that to him was the most important of all relationships. Van Buren is led into the most baffling kind of complexities because what the Gospels tell us of Jesus' conception of self makes it difficult to retain the son without the Father. But, says van Buren, we cannot speak of God at all—modern, empirically grounded man "cannot even speak analogically about 'God.'" [7] And so in the midst of his self-imposed restraints conflicting with his self-generated proclivities, he confronts the verse "He who has seen me has seen the Father." [8] The resultant "analysis" is necessarily so strained that it become almost ludicrous to one viewing it from the outside, sympathetic to the uses of linguistic analysis in appropriate frames of reference, but unburdened by a specific Christian commitment to retain the Gospel even in a supposed "secular meaning." This is what he says of Jesus' claim that one who has seen him "has seen the Father":

> The verification principle precludes taking this assertion of cosmological obedience as a straightforward empirical proposition. Its function is to say something about Jesus which we have already noticed in speaking of his freedom to make no claims for himself. We called attention then to the characteristics of humility, service, and living for other men. Undoubtedly, Jesus believed he was obeying some 'one', whom he called 'Father', but the Gospel of John, as well as the logic of language, forces us to silence before all questions concerning that 'one.' [9]

In the tortuous effort that van Buren must make because of his own need to have his Christological cake as well as eat it, one of the prime instances in which Jesus *does* make a specific claim for himself in terms of his most important relationship— "Do you not believe that I am in the Father and the Father in me?" [10]—is presented as evidence of Jesus' humility, and as "functioning" to say something of Jesus' "freedom to make no claims for himself"! Certainly, this Johannine passage, like

7 Paul M. van Buren, p. 64.
8 John 14:9.
9 Van Buren, p. 148.
10 John 14:10.

others, is open to many different interpretations—homiletical or exegetical. But van Buren does not claim to be preaching or interpreting. He pretends to be subjecting the Gospel to objective linguistic analysis acceptable to "modern, empirical man."

The defect is, of course, in his own peculiar mixture of "language games"—to use the jargon of which he is fond—not in his "blik" (a coined word—as if we did not have enough trouble with the words we already have—for a "fundamental attitude" that "is not achieved by empirical inquiry.") [11] He is, in fact, holding on to two conflicting "bliks," one of which is his response to Christian tradition and the person of Jesus, the other his serious attachment to language analysis as a method by which the New Testament message can be sustained. Thus he is forced to affirm that "the Easter *kerygma*" has meaning and we *may* talk about it, but that the "empiricist in us finds the heart of the difficulty not in what is said about God, but in the very talking about God at all." [12] But if the word "God" must, to be useful, point only to "verifiable fact," then the *kerygma*— which is essentially, and before rationalization, the announcement of the good news of Jesus' resurrection—and the idealized person of Jesus must also point to "verifiable facts."

Those who mix two standards of judgment in this fashion regarding what we may or may not speak of are, at the least, carelessly inequitable and, at the worst, impermissibly ingenious. Or perhaps some of them are being disingenuous, like Nikita Khrushchev when he made his satirical observation that though the Russian astronauts had probed "space" they had not found "God." They are displaying the graceless result of the effort to be unrelievedly "empirical."

Language has functions other than the "empirical," however, and the path of laboratory testing is, as we have already observed, not the only path to truth. Indeed, there is more than one kind of "truth." The operational function of language is vital in its proper area—the language that we use to convey instructions, for example, must be exact. If we want to say "Turn the

[11] Van Buren, p. 84.
[12] Van Buren, p. 84.

blue lever to the right" we must be utterly precise in our semantic, lest God forbid, we turn it to the left, or mistake the red
for the blue!

When we deal with problems of value or relationship, we can
no longer use operational terminology. Indeed, we must frequently use words that are more than words: "charged symbols"
is what Susanne Langer calls them. They are charged in the
same way a battery is charged; they are filled with power. They
have layers upon layers of associations, and they frequently have
depth connotations. But we do not discard them because of their
enriched character. In the language of inspiration they become
even more valuable.

Supreme among such words is the word "God." I am not
speaking of the Anglo-Germanic term alone, but of that word
and its equivalents in all the languages of men—all of which
seek to point to the same inexpressible reality. It is a word that,
contrary to what Harvey Cox has said, is more than the "linch-
pin" of Christendom,[13] for it expresses the outreach of millions
upon millions of non-Christians. And if van Buren may seek to
understand *kerygma* in terms that will not outrage the reason of
modern man, we may seek to understand "God" in modern
terms.

For the word "God" speaks of *both* value and relationship. It
represents our straining toward an ultimate source of value, and
it stands for the relationship that encompasses all relationships.
Nor should we ascribe a primitive naïveté to those who have in
the past used that heavily charged vocable or its equivalents in
other names. Whatever the language chopper might do to the
great theophany in Exodus 33, it points to a reality that is an
aspect of human experience and that is inaccessible to operational language:

> Moses said, "I pray Thee, show me Thy glory [the Hebrew word
> is *"Kavod,"* that aspect of the Divine that in Isaiah 6 is said to
> fill the entire world]." And He said, "I will make all my goodness
> pass before you, and will proclaim before you My name 'The

13 Harvey Cox, p. 244.

Lord' . . . But," He said, "you cannot see My face; for man shall
not see Me and live." [14]

This is a passage in which the Biblical writers sought to express the sense of mystery that inhered in the *fact* of Encounter.
The new insights that Moses brought to the people of Israel were
real. The experience was *real*. The source of those insights and
the manner in which they burst upon the world are shrouded in
mystery. Although these ancient writers lived in a pretechnical,
prescientific culture, we should credit them with no less intelligence than we have. They knew they were using a metaphorical
form of expression, that they were speaking of an ineffable God
who could not be described. When they said that God's "face"
could not be seen, they were giving utterance to the feeling that
He was manifest only in the traces of His being, the manifestations of His action, His "goodness." They were seeking to evoke
in words the awe-stricken response of the people to a moment
of unutterable significance. Expressive as the language was, they
knew it could not encompass the whole of the experience. It
could but lift the hem.

There are, we are saying, levels of relationship and aspects
of experience that are more direct—indeed, more "real"—than
verbal communication, and to express which mere language,
and especially exact language, are inadequate. Indeed, they
evaporate under linguistic analysis or psychological analysis.
Make the effort to describe with scientific exactitude the relationship of a young mother to the infant at her breast. Not only
will you bog down in physiological terminology about glandular
activity, stimulus and response, but you will miss the essential
meaning of the situation. That meaning yields itself up, even if
only partially, to "soft-focus" language, to poetry and to art.

Analytic techniques are, of course, essential in their appropriate frames of reference. They are necessary to the exploration of the relationship between words and the meanings that
the words seek to express. They are vital in the search for the
origins of mental states. But they cannot—in their present rudi-

[14] Exodus 33:18–20.

mentary forms—encompass the realities they presume to ana-
lyze.

Take as an example, on a popular level, that "instinctive" response of affection or affinity that is found in the history of lyric
poetry and of song: when across a crowded room somehow you
know . . . What the plain sense of the ordinary man testifies to
is that there is a total response that conditions language.

The inarticulate lover or mystic is neither talking nonsense
nor trying to "eff" the ineffable. He *is* trying to express what in
its deepest sense is inexpressible—and he is led by his need into
metaphor and poetry. To communicate his experience of relationship, he must use "depth language" or "expressive language," not the "steno-language" of analysis.[15]

The experience of "love at first sight" *can* be described in
steno-language. One might say of such a happening: "As each
physical form was registered through the optic nerve of the other
in the brain of the other, an associative or memory context was
stimulated that produced in each a slightly higher blood pressure
and quicker pulse rate. . . ." In a sense this is what happens—
but how it misses what *really* happens! There is much more
truth, with all its errors of fact, in "stout Cortez . . . with eagle
eyes" gazing on the Pacific, "Silent, upon a peak in Darien."

The literalist and the language chopper, because of this fact
of verbal life, not only fail to represent the truth when they must
deal with expressive or depth language, they actually *falsify*. I
often recall with affection and amusement the analysis that one
of my teachers made of the fourth verse in the Eighty-fourth
Psalm:

> Yea, the sparrow hath found a house, and
>   the swallow a nest for herself,
> Where she may lay her young;
> Even Thine altars, O Lord of Hosts,
> My King and my God!

Quite earnestly he would tell the class, "Obviously, something
is missing. Altars are not nesting-places for birds!" Obviously,

---

[15] Wheelwright's terms, *The Burning Fountain*, pp. 25–29.

something was missing, but it was not a scribal error. What was missing was the professor's capacity to respond to the metaphorical intention of the Biblical poet. The poet was not concerned with ornithology but with evoking the feeling of tenderness and security. The result of even this limited insensitivity was error. There is close correspondence between the errors made by literalist critics in interpreting the Bible, and the errors made by positivists in interpreting depth experience and depth language. "The positivist assumptions and vocabulary," says Philip Wheelwright, "are as inapplicable to poetry as an axe would be to woodcarving. The result . . . is splinters." [16]

The prosaic mind frequently misses the truth; and the prosaic mind is handicapped today, victimized by that culture lag of which we have spoken. The world of constructs in which the new physics dwells has to make do without working models. In the complex universe it reveals, we can no longer find the entire truth in formulas. There is a More, to which we must respond.

There is another form of experience more fundamental than language in the sense that it is antecedent to language and independent of it, and which is less open to cavil than situations that involve likes and dislikes, physical attractions and repulsions, in that in such an experience these factors may be absent, as gesture, and expression, and glance are absent. It is that *presentness* and *receptiveness* that are essential to dialogue in the sense in which Martin Buber uses that much-abused word. For Buber describes a situation where there is neither word nor overt sense contact, and yet relationship is established. That such a level of relationship may exist will be testified to only by those who have experienced it. But those who have known it (and who receive its description as what Buber calls "amici," in open, friendly receptiveness) will recognize it as prior to and hence more "real" than anything psychology may have to say about the "process" that has occurred. This is the event presented by Buber:

> Imagine two men sitting beside one another in any kind of solitude of the world. They do not speak with one another, they do

[16] Wheelwright, p. 38.

not look at one another, not once have they turned to one another. They are not in one another's confidence, the one knows nothing of the other's career, early that morning they got to know one another in the course of their travels. In this moment neither is thinking of the other; we do not need to know what their thoughts are. The one is sitting on the common seat obviously after his usual manner, calm, hospitably disposed to everything that may come. His being seems to say it is too little to be ready, one must also be really there. The other, whose attitude does not betray him, is a man who holds himself in reserve, withholds himself. But if we know about him we know that a childhood's spell is laid on him, that his withholding of himself is something other than an attitude, behind all attitude is entrenched the impenetrable inability to communicate himself. And now—let us imagine that this is one of the hours which succeed in bursting asunder the seven iron bands about our heart—imperceptibly the spell is lifted. But even now the man does not speak a word, does not stir a finger. Yet he does something. The lifting of the spell has happened to him—no matter from where—without his doing. But this is what he does now: he releases in himself a reserve over which only he himself has power. Unreservedly communication streams from him, and the silence bears it to his neighbor. Indeed it was intended for him, and he receives it unreservedly as he receives all genuine destiny that meets him. He will be able to tell no one, not even himself, what he has experienced. What does he now 'know' of the other? No more knowing is needed. For where unreserve has ruled, even wordlessly, between men, the word of dialogue has happened sacramentally.[17]

The experience of prelinguistic communication and the establishment of positive or negative relationship through gesture and facial expression has less depth significance than the experience that Buber describes, but it is more easily recognizable. It is akin to your dog's growl or his tail-wagging. But it is more than that. The nuances of *human* gesture are many, and they are invested with the meanings made possible by man's symbol-creating capacity. A shrugged shoulder may mean "I don't know" or, with only the slightest of physical changes, "I don't

[17] Martin Buber, *Between Man and Man* (New York: The Macmillan Company, 1965), p. 3.

care"—and sometimes the gesture or grimace conveys more
than the words. An old Yiddish joke, displaying that ability of
humor to point to more than its wordplay, presents a picture of
the distinctively human character of this kind of communication.
Two old friends meet on the street, and as each puts to the other
the conventional, bromidic questions ("How goes it?" "How is
your wife?" "What's new?") the other responds with distinctive
Yiddish-associated gestures, lip and face movements, and non-
verbal ejaculations ("Mnyeh!" "Phsss!" "Tch!"). This goes on
for about five minutes, and, as they are about to part, one grasps
the other's hand, pumps it, and says with enthusiastic sincerity,
"Nu! It's good for old friends to meet and speak out what's on
their hearts [*ausredem dem hertz*—have a heart-to-heart talk]!"

Words, then, are not the only barriers to understanding, and
the barriers between man and man, as well as between man and
significance, must be breached with something antecedent to
words—but how ineluctable is our dependence on words in our
effort to understand, to communicate our understanding, and
to find the key to relationship! Language is the most precious
mark of our human estate:

> Language is, without a doubt, the most momentous and at the
> same time the most mysterious product of the human mind. Be-
> tween the clearest animal call of love or warning or anger, and a
> man's least, trivial *word,* there lies a whole day of Creation—or
> in modern phrase, a whole chapter of evolution.[18]

The French scientist and religious thinker, Father Teilhard
de Chardin,[19] whose total insights may well herald a revolution
of Copernican importance in modern thought, surprisingly fails
to take account of the role of language. What is the point of
"hominisation," a word he coined to designate the evolutionary
emergence of that wondrous complex we call human? For him
it lies in the miracle of man's consciousness that he is conscious,
not only that he knows, but that he *knows* that he knows. This

[18] Langer, p. 103. The whole of Chapter 5, "Language," is relevant.
[19] Pierre Teilhard de Chardin, *The Phenomenon of Man* (New York:
Harper & Brothers, 1961).

he describes as a folding-back analogous to what takes place physically in the evolutionary and genetic process.

But my cat may well be conscious that he is conscious. His level of consciousness is not accessible to me. Certainly, he is alert to my changes of mood in a way that demonstrates his primary concern for his self-interest. The distinctive mark of man, the moment of "hominisation," is in the magic of the word. I am not only conscious of my consciousness but I can *say* it. I can say "I" and thus distinguish clearly my "I" from your "You." I can make a word into a symbol. I can conceptualize.

It is this wonder that Lewisohn records in his book *The Magic Word,* when he writes:

> All speech is purest incantation
> Summoning forth the heart of things,
> As on the morning of creation
> The magic word both says and sings.[20]

Why does language make so great a difference? The answer lies in that previously mentioned capacity of the word to serve as a symbol. It not only points—or "says"; it also expresses—or "sings." Animal cries or animal gestures are signs of association and recognition. Language begins "when sound keep its reference beyond the situation of its instinctive utterance." "Yum yum" may signify the presence of bananas, says Langer, but cries like "yum yum . . . cannot be used between meals to talk over the merits of the feast." [21]

A chimpanzee knows how to take a box and place it under a stalk of bananas that would otherwise be out of his reach—but he can do so only when both the box and the bananas are present to his sight at the same time. He is unable to bear in mind the concept of a "box" or of a "banana." Man can hold the concept in his mind, can look at the banana, think of a box and search for one—and there is reason to believe that man's ability to hold on to the concept is linked with the fact that he possesses

20 Ludwig Lewisohn, *The Magic Word* (New York: Farrar Straus, 1950), p. v.
21 Langer, p. 105.

a special key for association. He can say "box"—he has the *word*.[22]

The miraculous power of speech is most poignantly conveyed in Helen Keller's deeply moving account of the ecstasy of the moment when that key was placed in her hand—when she first took possession of a word and learned that it was a word. Susanne Langer tells us that the child, Helen Keller, had used "signs," had formed associations, learned to expect things, identified people and places. Language, as such, comes into being and the distinctively human is born when the sign becomes a symbol. For Helen Keller, that moment occurred when she discovered "that a certain datum in her limited sense-world had a *denotation,* that a particular act of her fingers constituted a *word*. This event had required a long preparation; the child had learned many finger acts, but they were as yet a meaningless play. Then one day, her teacher took her out to walk—and there the great advent of Language occurred." [23]

> She brought me my hat [the memoir reads] and I knew I was going out into the warm sunshine. This thought, if a wordless sensation may be called a thought, made me hop and skip with pleasure.
>
> We walked down the path to the well-house, attracted by the fragrance of the honeysuckle with which it was covered. Some one was drawing water and my teacher placed my hand under the spout. As the cool stream gushed over my hand she spelled into the other the word *water,* first slowly, then rapidly. I stood still, my whole attention fixed upon the motion of her fingers. Suddenly I felt a misty consciousness as of something forgotten—a thrill of returning thought; and somehow the mystery of language was revealed to me. I knew then that w–a–t–e–r meant the wonderful cool something that was flowing over my hand. That living word awakened my soul, gave it light, hope, joy, set it free! There were barriers still, it is true, but barriers that in time could be swept away.
>
> I left the well-house eager to learn. Everything had a name, and each name gave birth to a new thought. As we returned to

[22] Langer, pp. 126–135. Based on the researches of Yerkes and Köhler.
[23] Langer, p. 62.

the house every object which I touched seemed to quiver with life. That was because I saw everything with the strange, new sight that had come to me.[24]

After sharing this experience, so eloquently recorded, with any degree of empathy, one can never again say "only a word" or speak of "mere words." Here is the heart of the human miracle. Helen Keller had discovered in the simplest and most direct way that language has a symbolic quality. She had known the word "water" as a "sign." It meant that one was thirsty, or that the object that it designated was present. Suddenly, she learned that the *word* could be retained, that it could point to a concept or idea of water, that it could be remembered and become the subject of *thought*.

Words for Helen Keller had to be converted into a complicated system of tactile sensations—but even without the wonder of sound the mystery and the magic of the word were not denied her. The word "both says and sings," both designates and expresses. In its double power, it makes possible beauty, and action and thought, art, science, and philosophy. Without what has been called his symbol-making capacity, man would not be "human." All that we like to think of as man's accomplishments, his achievements in the mastery of techniques, in the description of his world, in sharpened consciousness and the search for meaning, would not have been possible without language. In his drive to express himself, he has invented other "languages"; expressive in music and the visual arts, and designative in mathematics, logic, and engineering. He has found the means to express the inspirational content of his thought in poems and prayers, in symphonies and paintings, and to record and advance his operational thought in formulas and blueprints and maps, in theories and reasoned proofs.

But the virtues of language, like those of all great "gifts" entrusted to man, depend upon its use. The barriers do not begin in words; but words are used to harden them, to provide the secondary defenses that make them more inaccessible. For words

[24] Helen Keller, *The Story of My Life* (Garden City: Doubleday, Doran & Co., 1936), pp. 23–24.

can be snares and pitfalls. They may be used in conscious irresponsibility in propaganda and distortion, they can become ambivalent, slippery, and two-faced, so that men working with them may fail in both expression and designation.

The fundamentalist religionist who says "truth" is referring to a different complex from that which is in the mind of a physicist. The prosecuting attorney who says "justice" is not dealing with the same concept as that which is in the mind of a contemporary interpreter of the prophet Isaiah. The suburban householder who, caring for his lawn, says "turf" is designating something quite different from the "turf" entrusted to the keeper of a six-hundred-year-old British greensward.

Words are instruments. No one who has ever worked conscientiously with words could possibly underestimate the difficulty of making them unambiguous, of laboring to make them the vehicle of honest communication and expression. We confront incessantly the danger that we may use them poorly, for evil and not for good. For our verbal skills provide us with endless devices. They create our power to rationalize, to cover up, and to conceal. A proposition may be laid down in imagined exactitude, but its later interpretation is dependent upon attitude and mood. "Congress shall make no law respecting the establishment of religion," says the Constitution of the United States, but the defenders of the Constitution, the members of the Supreme Court, governed by their differing "philosophies" and outlooks, will draw differing conclusions from that seemingly simple phrase. "Thou shalt not kill" is a proposition to which the world gives almost unanimous assent, but does it or does it not refer to self-defense, war, capital punishment, or nuclear testing with its potential delayed killings through radiation poisoning?

Words are instruments. We have no choice but to use them— to be conscious of their inadequacies and to evoke as nearly as we can those realities that are antecedent to the words and for which the words are mustered and arranged.

"God" is also a word. As such, it is subject to all of the inadequacies of language and to its variant uses. It may even be,

as has been said, the most abused of all words. We must, therefore, labor to understand both the word and that to which it
gives expression. "God" is a word, but God is also the reality
to which the word seeks to point. This is how I understand Paul
Tillich's cryptic statement that "God is a symbol for God"—for
although it has the appearance of Delphic obscurity it is neither
gobbledygook nor nonsense syllables. God is met in the world
by limited, imperfect beings who can apprehend Him only as
person. The limitless ground of all being can be approached
only with limited finite language and with that limited comprehension that cannot even reach to the bounds of our physical
universe. The word "God" and the inadequately apprehended
God both *point beyond themselves* to that Lord of All over
against Whom we stand.

There are still those who can say "God," in this sense, who
can use the word with reverence and with rationality and who—
as we shall now see—can speak of God in contexts meaningful
to modern men, perhaps necessary to man's survival.

CHAPTER SIX

ATHEISM IS DEAD

Those who say that God is dead and who mean that the concept of God is no longer useful or intellectually viable provide us with terms for our consideration of atheism. If the rational foundations of atheism have been shattered, if its primary axioms are no longer credible, atheism is defunct even if it still claims followers and propagators.

We say that atheism is dead. In the form in which it has been expressed in our time it has rested either on the premise of materialism that nothing is real or significant except matter functioning according to predetermined law, or on the basis of scientism that nothing is provable or true except as determined by scientific method and that, moreover, scientific method has an all-inclusive competence. The certainty that used to mark such declarations has now evaporated.

The primary philosophical defender of materialistic atheism once was Marxism. But although millions of the faithful have not "heard" of it, the major preconceptions of Marxism, especially in the world of physics, have become obsolete.

Marxism, as philosophy and as epistemology, was founded upon confidence in the stability and basic character of matter—hence it is called "materialism," historical materialism or dialectical materialism. Engels, cofounder with Marx of the movement that sprang from his thinking, confidently states in *Anti-Dühring* that "matter without motion is as inconceivable as motion without matter." This confidence is the foundation stone of Marxist atheism. Modern physics has pulled the rug from under it. Matter and energy are, we have learned, interchangeable—at least, matter can be converted into energy ($E = MC^2$) and it is at least logically conceivable that energy could be converted into matter. The building blocks of matter now seem to be energy-systems rather than solid particles. The old distinctions have broken down.

What happens to a system of "historical materialism" when "matter" itself, which had appeared stable and permanently reliable, proves to have been deceptive and to be something quite different from that which it was conceived to be? The foundations of the system are jeopardized and until a new and satisfying rationalization can be formulated, the only possible response for the orthodox is denial and attack. The medieval church forced Galileo publicly to renounce his defense of the Copernican theory, and the Marxist-Leninist "church" of our own era has waged violent and nonscientific propaganda warfare against Mendelian genetics and Einsteinian physics. Soviet scientists are drawn into the battle and led to use the language of attack and vituperation when Marxist preconceptions are endangered by new knowledge or new insights. One extreme example—extreme but classic in its unwitting exposure of the technique that was used—is found in a resolution adopted at a meeting of astronomers in Leningard in 1948 and recorded in the official organ of the Soviet Academy of Science. The resolution called upon Soviet scientists to oppose the "reactionary-idealistic 'theory' of a finite widening of the universe." All relativistic conceptions, the resolution held, "should be regarded as a manifestation of cringing before the reactionary science of the bourgeois West. . . . It is necessary to expose tirelessly this astronomical idealism which helps clericalism. To counterbalance bourgeois cosmology, Soviet science must intensify its work on regions beyond our galaxy, to give a materialistic explanation of the red displacement in the spectra of galaxies and other phenomena." [1]

Like Galileo, offending scientists, and even offending artists and writers have been forced to recant. And if afterwards, they say *"eppur si muove"* (nevertheless, it does move)—as it is hoped Galileo did—it must be *sotto voce*.

[1] Harrison E. Salisbury, *New York Times*, July 14, 1949, p. 1.

Many former Marxists have recognized all this. The dramatic defections from "the Party" that occurred in the 1940's were not all because of disillusionment with the course of Soviet Communism and with the actual developments in the U.S.S.R. The disenchantment of such men as Ignazio Silone and Arthur Koestler was also the result of their conviction that reliance upon technique and manipulation was insufficient foundation for a meaningful world-view and that an amoral approach to the evaluation of means was inadequate in the realm of ethics.[2]

Koestler early understood the fallacy of Marxist reductionism. With Samuel Butler he proclaimed, "Nothing is ever *merely* anything." He left the party as much because of new spiritual insights as because of his revulsion against the absence of compassion and truth in the techniques of the party apparatus.

There are ways of knowing other than the scientific way, said Koestler. "The significance of our era," he wrote, "is that science has been forced by its own development to recognize its limitations, and thus to make room for the other way of knowing whose place it usurped for almost three centuries."[3]

For Koestler, that "other way" is tinged with Eastern mysticism. He calls it "contemplation." For Hayim Greenberg, a Jewish intellectual who was for decades one of the leaders of the Labor Zionist movement, the failure of Marxism lay in the fact that it sought to link its social vision with an absolute materialism. He came to understand that there is no necessary "logical interdependence between the conception of a purely mechanical universe where only simple particles move aimlessly, without guidance or design, and an ideal aiming at a planned and harmonious society."[4]

Greenberg was one of the first Jewish Marxists to turn back toward Jewish religion, but he was followed by an increasing flood of mellowed former anti-religious Socialists who swell

[2] See *The God That Failed,* ed. Richard H. S. Crossman (New York: Harper & Brothers, 1949).

[3] Arthur Koestler, *The Yogi and the Commissar* (New York: The Macmillan Company, 1945), p. 228.

[4] *The Inner Eye.* Selected Essays of Hayim Greenberg. (New York: Jewish Frontier Association, 1964), I, 246.

synagogue membership rolls today. One of his friends and colleagues who describes the special outlook of Hayim Greenberg really writes of hosts of others, less sophisticated and articulate, but similarly motivated:

"Greenberg was a socialist but if one reads his 'Notes on Marxism' or his 'To a Communist Friend' one sees how basic were his differences with Marxism, differences going far beyond the excesses of the Russian dictatorship. Greenberg's view of man's soul was too complex to enable him to accept the fairy-tale simplicity of the Marxist version of man's motives and needs. In his anti-Communism Greenberg was never, like so many liberals, a disillusioned fellow-traveler turned sour by evidence of unsavory practice in the Socialist Fatherland. Greenberg's opposition was more fundamental. His conception of socialism had to allow not only for the analysis of Marx but of Freud, and it had to include the illumination of religion." [5]

Will Herberg is another who has given literate leadership to this trend. Once a member of the Young Communist League and an editor of publications of the Communist Party, U.S.A., he is now professor of religion at Drew University and the author of an important work on Judaism's message for today.[6] Herberg in his Marxist career had accepted the expectation that "through its own inherent energies, the materialistic dialectic of history would sooner or later solve every problem, fulfill every possibility and eliminate every evil of human life . . ." but he came to affirm the antithetical view. [7]

Put to the test, the Marxist faith failed. It proved itself incapable of explaining the facts or sustaining the values that gave meaning to life, the very values it had itself enshrined as its ultimate goals.

This is similar to the analysis of Marxism's failure by Albert Camus, who at his death was voicing an expectation of new and redemptive developments in the search for a foundation for hu-

[5] Marie Syrkin, in her "Foreword" to *The Inner Eye,* I, xiii.

[6] Will Herberg, *Judaism and Modern Man* (New York: Harper & Row, 1955).

[7] Will Herberg, "From Marxism to Judaism," *Commentary,* Vol. III, No. 1 (January 1948), pp. 25 ff.

mane values, but who knew deeply the inability of Marxism to provide that foundation. His judgment of Marxist prophecies finds Marxism wanting in its economics, its science, and its philosophical formulations.[8] Marx, he says, was far greater than what his disciples made of Marxism, for Marx made ethical demands in behalf of humanity; he taught that "when work is a degradation, it is not life" and thus defended the dignity of man; and he proclaimed of ends and means "An end that requires unjust means is not a just end." [9] But Marx destroys all transcendence and by seeking to draw values only from time and facts and events replaces good and evil with duty and thus frighteningly justifies his cynical and amoral successors. Camus writes:

"But every kind of socialism is Utopian. Utopia replaces God by the future. Then it proceeds to identify the future with ethics; the only values are those which serve this particular future. For that reason Utopias have almost always been coercive and authoritarian." [10]

This and the fact that an imagined end of history introduces into history a value "foreign to history" and "foreign to ethics"— a "dogma without foundation" which becomes "an arbitrary and terroristic principle"—bring us to understand why "the history of Russian Communism gives the lie to every one of its principles."

"Once more we find . . . metaphysical rebellion, which, this time, advances to the clash of arms and the whispering of passwords, but forgetful of its real principles, burying its solitude in the bosom of armed masses, covering the emptiness of its negations with obstinate scholasticism, still directed to the future, which it has made its only god, but separated from it by a multitude of nations that must be overthrown and continents that must be dominated." [11]

[8] See Albert Camus, *The Rebel* (New York: Vintage Books, 1960), pp. 210–226.
[9] *The Rebel*, pp. 208–209.
[10] *The Rebel*, p. 208.
[11] *The Rebel*, pp. 224, 226.

And so we stand, "with weapons in our hands and a lump in our throats." [12]

This is the twilight area that is occupied by many contemporary scientists and intellectuals. They stand between two worlds, "one dead the other powerless to be born." They are far more certain of their selected affirmations than they are of sweeping negations. For this very reason, they speak with a new humility and with a hint of an ever-present nostalgia for conviction. Henry Margenau, for example, is able to talk about a "transcendence out of the domain of science into a region from which science as a whole can be surveyed," as he writes:

> . . . I see nothing in the methodology of science which forbids this expansion, this extrapolation upon the method of science. Most scientists readily admit that their methods have limits and that beyond these limits procedures controlled by other principles may well take hold.[13]

For many scientists, the fact that science deals with probabilities and makes no claim to absolute or final truth makes atheism as untenable as any traditional theological view.

This is the position of Hudson Hoagland, who rejects any line of connection between traditional religious affirmations and the origin of ethical values but roundly declares, "The existence of God can neither be proved nor disproved, and honest agnosticism becomes the only answer for some of us in spite of the will to believe." [14]

In the words, "in spite of the will to believe," the nostalgia for conviction is acknowledged. It exists today not only among agnostic men of science but among hosts of plain people who enter houses of worship hoping for something to happen, wishing they could believe, conscious of a yawning emptiness in their lives. They yearn for some organizing principle, some affirmation that will bring them meaning and direction even as they sink

[12] *The Rebel*, p. 8.

[13] Henry Margenau, "Truth in Science and Religion" in *Science Ponders Religion*, ed. Harlow Shapley (New York: Appleton-Century-Crofts, Inc., 1960), p. 111.

[14] Hudson Hoagland, "Some Reflections on Science and Religion," in *Science Ponders Religion*, p. 24.

themselves in obligations, job, communal activity, and in play that is frequently a feverishly tense quest for relaxation. They strive to blot out the emptiness, to forget it. They share in the great loneliness of modern man, in the fear that no-one cares, that in Wordsworth's words "such emptiness at length seems at the heart of all things."

But they manage to bury that nostalgia. "We are modern and emancipated!" And "Oh well, most enlightened and successful people today are just as indifferent as I am. If they do not reject religion entirely, they make a formal bow in its direction just as infrequently as I do."

And yet, the emptiness remains. Atheism was at least a conviction on which to build one's life. Agnosticism is as shaky a foundation as that which existed in the mind of the poor demented physicist who took to wearing huge, padded boots for fear that he would fall through the insubstantial structure of energy and "onta" on which he walked.

Our thesis is that we can respond to the great final questions of life with a set of convictions that will not outrage reason, that the yearning or nostalgia can be satisfied without dishonor to the modern self-image.

We may not expect simplicity or finality. No one who deals with the basic life questions which are religion's concern may shirk their agonizing profundity. To approach religious belief without respect for the tensions and the difficulties of the search for meaning is "to delude ourselves, or to reduce faith to insignificance, to an ailment of childhood, which one must get over as soon as possible."

Yet millions still speak in terms of total reverence for scientific method and millions still speak in Marxist terms whether its hypotheses have been proved obsolete or not. This is so because of the intrinsic nature of human intellectual development where man's emotional and evaluational stance changes much more slowly than does the content of his technical or physical knowledge.

There is always a lag between the uncovering of new knowledge and its embodiment in man's cultural orientation.

Henry Margenau helps us understand this by distinguishing between two distinct "movements" in the progress of thought. He calls the first of these, "the obvious movement." It is the movement of progress that takes place in facts and in techniques—the movement from discovery to application. The other movement, which Margenau calls "the obscure movement," is the movement of progress toward a world-view adequate to the new knowledge.[15] The first movement—the obvious, technological, factual movement—moves far more rapidly than the second movement—the development of ideas, or of philosophical thought. And today the obvious movement is moving more rapidly than ever.

Newton discovered the laws of classical mechanics—mechanistic physics—in the seventeeth century and, says Margenau, the machine age began in the late eighteenth and the early nineteenth centuries. More than a hundred years had to elapse between discovery and application. Today, discoveries that are made in the new physics find their technological application as early as ten years after the discovery has been made. Radar, electronic devices, new missile devices, new fantastic technological developments—they are all being developed at an extremely rapid pace once the discovery of the scientific facts makes them possible.

The second movement—the development of a world-view—has always taken longer. From the time of Kepler and his astronomical discoveries to the time of Immanuel Kant and his philosophy fitting the Keplerian-Copernican universe, there was a lapse of 150 years.

Most of us are still living in the fact-bound universe of fifty to seventy-five years ago: the universe of positivism, of "scientism," even the universe of Newtonian physics. We must learn to live with a world-view adequate to encompass factual knowledge and an understanding of the world of the new physics.

We have already mentioned the appearance in our time of a new type of scientific humility. Those who have penetrated most

[15] See Henry Margenau, *Open Vistas* (New Haven: Yale University Press, 1961), pp. 39 ff.

deeply into the unknown are frequently those most impressed by aspects of reality that defy common sense and the formal logic of an earlier age. The revelations of modern science offer support to those who stand in reverence before the wonder of all-that-is. Let me offer some examples of such revelations.

First, modern research has all but wiped away the distinction between life and nonlife; between the so-called organic, and the so-called inorganic; between rocks and fossils on the one hand and you and me on the other hand. The body in which you feel at home is an incalculable multiplicity of tiny cells, each independently alive; and yet the surface of every cell has room for hundreds of millions of protein molecules; the very protein molecules of which those cells are built. And the proteins, in turn, are composed of amino acids. At the University of Chicago, by sending an electric charge through gases, scientists have been able to create out of primary elements the amino acids that are the building blocks of life. These amino acids have recently been synthesized in the laboratory. What does this mean? Man has succeeded in imitating the process by which eons ago the first life emerged on this earth. If we say that growth is the property that distinguishes life from nonlife, we have to look at those viruses about which we hear so much as the causes of disease and which seem to be giant proteins. They propagate and they grow. What we call the genes, on which we hang so much of our genetic science, may very well be self-fermenting proteins. Indeed, one biologist goes so far as to say that the word "life" has not as yet entirely lost its usefulness. What it adds up to is this: From the atom to man, from man to the galaxies, the differences are not differences in ultimate nature; they are differences of scheme and of degree of complexity.

The second relevation is that the activity of all this basic stuff that constitutes all things, the whole of matter—can only be described by the word "purposive." This can be illustrated by the wonder of the process by which the embryo develops, the wonder of a child within its mother's womb. Two cells proliferating into many cells, the limb buds, which are to become the arms and the legs, suddenly appearing, and "all of the many cells acting, growing, organizing, seemingly by themselves, so that they look like a magnificently trained crew of workers."[16] Indeed, researchers in neuroanatomy at Yale University have indicated that in the development of the embryo, wave structure, a structure of *energy,* seems to precede physical structure."

A group of these growing, multiplying cells, "travel from the skin, to which they belong," settle down in a prepared cup; arrange themselves in a compact, suitable ball; "turn into transparent fibers, and make a lens of the right size, in the right place." In short, these cells "behave as if fairly possessed." What do they produce? Not only a lens in the right place, but a lens whose curvature is able to focus automatically on the near and the far; and a camera stop, the pupil of our eye, which is self-adjusting to the intensity of the light, something that we are only now beginning to imitate mechanically in our cameras. Sherrington, a scientist, not a preacher, also makes this statement: "We can only understand the organism if we regard it as produced under the guidance of *thought* for an *end.*"[17] Why do these cells behave as they do? The answer of Sherrington is that it can only be described as a *"final cause."* Job and the sages marveled at the eye. Shakespeare cried out, "What a piece of work is a man!" They did not know the half of it!

Third, to these new insights into the unity and the purposiveness of matter we must add the knowledge that the new physics brings us, knowledge of the interdependence of matter and energy, space and time. Einstein's last years were spent in the quest for a unified field theory that would explain the minuscule world of the atom, just as it would explain the vast and illimitable reaches of outer space: protons and electrons and the galaxies in one formula. Atom, man, and the furthest distances of our universe and the greatest aggregations of stars are but different aspects of the same comprehensive, coherent, planned unity. The quest is not completed, but the hypothesis is still pro-

[16] Charles Scott Sherrington, *Man on His Nature* (New York: Doubleday & Co., 1953). This description is taken from Chapter IV, especially pp. 120 ff.

[17] Sherrington, p. 127.

ductive, and it is aesthetically satisfying in a scientific sense.

Some "religion" and some "science" can never be reconciled. One cannot reconcile Darwin and his approach to the development of the species and of evolution, with Bishop Lightfoot, who categorically declared that no one must doubt that God or the Holy Trinity created man on a Friday in the year 4004 B.C., at 9 A.M.[18] But there is an area in which scientist and religionist, humanitarian intellectual and theologian stand together before the unknown, stand in a position where the only intelligent response, other than turning away and disregarding the problem, is the humility that eventuates in the reverent hypothesis and in the act of faith.

Scientific postulates, Margenau maintains, are no different in essence from what we call, in the field of ethics, ideals or norms, or what we call in the field of religion, faith. And he says, "I hasten to add that I can think of nothing surer than a tried scientific postulate or indeed an ideal that lights my way or a fervent religious conviction." [19]

We confront the unknown today in an unprecedented way. Science used to think that it could offer a definition of reality. Today, it knows that it does not know. This may not be so of all who have finished a course in elementary physics, where they have been introduced to a *mélange* of factual discoveries, but it is so of those who are in the vanguard of scientific exploration.

What is this desk upon which I write? Is it real? And if it is real, what is its reality? It responds to touch; you can hear it when I pound it; you see it—these are on the level of experience. We experience it as "real." But investigate its composition, look into the nature of the wood, determine the construction of the molecules, examine the atomic structure. What is in the atom? We used to say there were particles inside the atom. But a particle is something that you can use or throw, or accelerate or move. We have learned, however, that it does not act like a particle, because when you take one of these so-called elementary

---

[18] See Hayim Greenberg, *The Inner Eye* (New York: Jewish Frontier Association, 1953), p. 122.

[19] Margenau, p. 65.

particles and shoot it through an instrument or accelerate it up against a screen in which there are two holes you find that it goes through both holes at the same time!

This defies common sense. You cannot draw a picture of that or understand what happens. At one time, scientists said it was a "wave"; but it acted like a particle: you cannot accelerate waves. Then, they called it a "wavicle." Today, scientists have given up both terms. They speak of "onta"—the "elementary" particles of being—neutrons, electrons, protons, photons. These are the "onta," and more than a score of them are already catalogued.

I have said that this desk that I can hit and that you can see is made up of these "onta." What is the size and the shape and the position or the color of an electron? The researchers tell us these are nonsensical questions. They have no relevance. An electron has no position. It is nowhere at any time, and it means nothing to talk about its color or shape.

You can speak of the mass of an electron as it registers on an instrument, but from the standpoint of experience all that you know of the electron is that which registers—the plane of experience is the ray of light you see reflected from something that is making it, or the measurement of mass that you can get from something that is there. You begin to see how it acts, and you know what it is *not,* thus, you know that it is not a particle and it is not a wave. You can define it in negatives, and you can define it by its effects, but what is it? It is a statistical aggregate!

Reality, we are told by science today, inheres in probability. That is all that this desk is. It is an aggregate of probabilities, and those probabilities are convertible. The energy within the movement of those particles is convertible into matter; and matter is convertible, not theoretically, but actually, into that energy. This is what makes possible the atomic bomb or the hydrogen fusion bomb: the conversion of matter into pure energy.

Where is reality? Where are the materialistic, mechanistic bases of science that gave rise to Marxism? They are gone. This is what led Albert Einstein to offer his famous dictum when he was told that all we could say about electrons was to state the chances that they would be in a certain place at a certain time—probabilities like throwing dice. The faces on the sides of dice show numbers from one to six, and if you throw the dice a certain number of times, the laws of probability will bring up a seven or an eleven with a certain predictable frequency. Yet, there is freedom in the way in which the dice will fall. Einstein reacted against this analogy and made his famous statement: "God does not play dice with the universe." Within these areas of probability and chance, there are laws that in the larger world of desks and planets and of stars and of galaxies function with regularity. Conversely, there is freedom amid the sequential unfolding of the universe.

Another area of the unknown is the dark and hidden country of what both psychiatrists and religionists must, for lack of a better word, call the soul—that developing consciousness that marks all evolution; that area of hidden thought within us linking us to all consciousness and all life—that driving will to meaning that contemporary existential psychiatry holds to be more important than the will to pleasure or the will to power.

Man in the new science is not the detached spectator of an objective universe. He is part of the whole, acting upon it and being acted upon by it in turn. Modern science provides us with support for the belief that our intelligence, our hopes, and our emotions are not lonely, chance phenomena. They are, rather, those aspects of the whole that we are able to perceive consciously. Modern scientific knowledge does not contradict the belief that memory, foresight, planning, the insights into good and evil, and the ideals to which man at his best has ever aspired, are present in the cosmos. They are written, so to speak, into the very constitution of the universe.

We are all possessed by inhibitions that we inherit from the so-called age of reason. Many of us admit to "feeling silly" when we use words like "God" and "soul." This was the expression used by Dr. George Nakhnikian, of Wayne State University, who said he "felt silly" because of his cosmic gratitude in a

certain situation. He would have felt silly if he had gone to his
Armenian Church to light a candle or had given money to the
priest to give to the poor.[20] But if we "feel silly" when we talk
about God or when we talk about the soul or when we talk
about meaning, we may well "feel silly" because we do not know
enough, because we are caught in a culture lag.

Of the two movements that I have described, the obvious
movement and the obscure movement—the growth of factual
knowledge and the slower growth of a world-view adequate to
that knowledge—the second movement is beginning to express
itself in a ferment from which a new vision may emerge. It is at
least certain that our new scientific knowledge does not provide
a basis for materialism, or for positivism, or for mechanism, or
for atheism. The new knowledge cannot, indeed, be reconciled
with any one of them.

"The sea of faith" that Matthew Arnold, in the late nineteenth century, saw as emptying out and running down "the
naked shingles of the world" may today be filling once again.
The more we know, the more we find of the need for reverence.
An insight to which William Wordsworth gives utterance is not
foreign to the mood of Sherrington, or Margenau, or Greenberg.
For Wordsworth expresses the new scientific humility when he
writes:

. . . And I have felt
A presence that disturbs me with the joy
Of elevated thoughts; a sense sublime
Of something far more deeply interfused,
Whose dwelling is the light of setting suns,
And the round ocean and the living air,
And the blue sky, and in the mind of man:
A motion and a spirit, that impels
All thinking things, all objects of all thought
And rolls through all things. . . .

This is the Cosmic Whole to which we may also turn as we
say "God."

20 George Nakhnikian, "On the Cognitive Import of Certain Conscious
States," in *Religious Experience and Truth,* ed. Sidney Hook (New York:
New York University Press, 1961), p. 161.

CHAPTER SEVEN

THE WIDENED HORIZONS

We have found in the new science support for a position of openness toward religious knowledge. This is the antithesis of the assumption frequently made that the revelations of contemporary science must be shattering to the "faithful." When Dr. Harlow Shapley, the astronomer, was the guest of our synagogue some years ago, he disclosed traces of that attitude. With a mixture of frankness and puckishness, he expressed surprise that he had been invited to speak in a house of worship—the invitation upset his preconceptions of parochialism and narrowness in all institutions of religion. He contended that when, during the Darwin centennial, in a panel with leading theologians he had suggested a discussion of the transformation of religion under the impact of science, the chairman had adjourned the meeting.

His subsequent generalization from this instance, while in error, is certainly not uncommon. The word "religion" covers such a broad spectrum of meanings, however, that it is unfair to associate it only with stubborn imperviousness to reason or established fact. But the propensity to generalize grows out of the tendency to categorize in either-or fashion. It is easy—even if incorrect—to set humanism against theism, naturalism against "supernaturalism," and openness against dogmatism and to associate "religion," in each instance, with the latter term.

Even an astronomer isolated in the purity of his observatory tower would not be likely to impute a "will to blindness" to religionists today. This is one of the positive popular effects of the radical statements of religious problems in the "God is dead" debate. Religious leadership is confronting the "new knowledge" and responding to it. By that new knowledge the odds are made overwhelming that man is not the kingpin and summit of all creation that both Biblical faith and nineteenth-century humanism had confidently made him out to be. Shapley would have us accept that new knowledge and adjust to it in "new attitudes toward religion and philosophy." [1] In this he resembles Margaret Fuller, who is said to have proclaimed, "I accept the universe," a statement to which Thomas Carlyle reportedly rejoined, "By God, she'd better!"

There are four primary revelations of contemporary astronomy that Shapley would have us accept:

1. Given the basic hydrogen atoms that are the "building blocks of the universe," all natural phenomena could have evolved without any assistance from the "supernatural" and, indeed, undoubtedly did so evolve. As for how it all began, "the field is open for theories of creation," said Shapley. Two of them are leading contenders for acceptance in the scientific world today. One is the so-called "big bang" theory of the late Abbé LeMaître, which posits a primeval atom that exploded ten thousand million years ago. The other is the "constant state" theory whose chief exponent has been Fred Hoyle, that the universe is always being created: as it expands, new atoms of hydrogen are continually coming into being. The rate is no more than one atom in a mass the size of a terrestrial skyscraper in every twenty-four-hour period, but the universe is so vast that even at this rate billions of hydrogen atoms are coming into being at every moment. (It should be added that more recent discoveries in the field of quasars, or quasi-stellar masses, suggest new support for the "big bang" and have forced Hoyle to do some rigorous new thinking.[2] These new discoveries suggest the metaphysically disturbing possibility that we may live in a "pulsating universe" that begins in a "big bang," expands for forty-one

[1] "Stars, Ethics and Survival," in *Science Ponders Religion*, ed. Harlow Shapley (New York: Appleton-Century-Crofts, Inc., 1960), p. 11.

[2] See Fred Hoyle, *Galaxies, Nuclei and Quasars* (New York: Harper & Row, 1965).

billion years, then contracts for forty-one billion years to the point of a new explosion, after which the whole horrendous process takes place all over again. The Kohelet-like implications of this theory—"that which has been will be . . . and there is nothing new under the sun" and "all things toil to weariness"— disturbing as they are, demand further exploration.)

2. The sun is not the center of the universe. Indeed, we are inhabitants of a relatively insignificant planet, number three of a tiny star that is on the outer reaches of the Milky Way, our own galaxy, some 30,000 light-years away from its center. And our Milky Way is but one of millions of galaxies spread out through what Shapley calls the "meta-galaxy," the universe as we know it.

3. We are not the only thinking or sentient beings in the universe. By a conservative estimate, there are undoubtedly at least one hundred million planets that sustain life at least as fully developed as our own. It may be very different from our own life: we happen to have evolved with backbones. We stand up straight. On other planets, they may be globs of multicellular life and other forms of which we cannot even conceive. But the likelihood is that if there are globs, they are globs with greater intelligence than our own.

4. The observable universe, that is, the universe that we can see with our largest telescopes, and dream of seeing with our most perfect telescopes, is not the *All;* it is not the totality of being. Indeed, it is possible, without violating the canons of scientific thought, to imagine our meta-galaxy—namely, all that we can detect out to a distance of a billion light-years and all that we can posit out to a distance of two billion light-years— as but part of a larger system. It is not beyond the range of possibility that this meta-galaxy, of which we are such a tiny part, may in turn be an atom in a system that is to our meta-galaxy as our meta-galaxy (the macrocosm) is to the atoms within it (microcosm).[3] The possibility that all this vastness is but a tiny

[3] Harlow Shapley, *Of Stars and Men* (Boston: Beacon Press, 1958), especially p. 114.

atom of something incalculably more vast sounds like the most fantastic science fiction. But the possibility exists.

What conclusions are we to draw from these revelations? If all this is so and if we insist on using the word "God," then we must recognize the foolishness of any effort to localize the concern of that God in one corner of the universe. We must learn that it is both presumptuous and ridiculous of us to believe that we are the summit of creation and that we are the major focus of Divine interest.

I can understand that these revelations would, if accepted, be profoundly disturbing to some forms of religion. They would shatter the simple fundamentalist who reads his Bible as if it were a scientific textbook. It would shatter the believers in a three-story universe, a universe constructed as our Bible and most prayer books poetically picture it: of a heaven and an earth and some kind of underworld beneath the earth. And these revelations would be shattering to one who believes with simple naïveté that Jesus was the only begotten son of God and that his appearance on this earth, some 1,970 years ago, was the midpoint of *all* history.

But these revelations would not be shattering to any faith, Jewish, or Christian, or Eastern, that recognizes the limitations of human knowledge, that expresses humility, and that stands in awe of the total reality. To those who have such a faith, the discoveries of contemporary astronomy, as presented to us by Shapley, will be exciting and stimulating. They will motivate the search for new orientations. But they will not be shattering.

The writer of the Book of Job would not have shrunk from the revelations of contemporary astronomy. How he would have welcomed the added testimony of a Harlow Shapley, for the added depth and power it would have given to his sense of man's tininess as he confronts the vastness of the universe! He strove mightily to express it through the mythologies and the limited science of his own time. When he said "Where wast thou, when I laid the foundations of the earth, when the morning stars sang together and all the sons of God shouted for joy," and when he said "Canst thou bind the chains of the

Pleiades or loose the bands of Orion? "Knowest thou the ordinances of the heavens?" [4] when he used all the symbols of complexity and of grandeur that he could muster from the world of nature and of the experience of man—how we would have welcomed these additional words with which to express his sense of the wonder of the universe!

The Psalmist who sang, "When I behold thy heavens, the work of thy fingers, the moon and stars which thou hast created, what is man, that thou art mindful of him, or the son of man that thou thinkest of him?" [5] would not have been shattered. When he wrote those words, he thought that the stars were only 8,000 naked-eye objects, the stars that could be identified without a telescope. If he had known that the universe that we can observe contains a number of stars described by the figure 10^{20}— one hundred thousand million billion stars—it would have added strength to his argument!

It would not have shattered the faith of the Talmudic period. How did they explain this phrase "When I behold thy heavens . . . the work of thy fingers?" They said: [6] "It follows from this phrase that the heavens filled with His glory still contain *no more of Him* than one could find in a single touch of the finger of the Holy One, Blessed Be He." (*"Kiv'yochol,"* they would add—"speaking metaphorically.")

This is why I feel that a question put by Fred Hoyle is meaningless in the context of my faith. Hoyle asks if it is reasonable to believe that it was given to the Hebrews to understand mysteries far deeper than anything that we can comprehend.

In relation to Judaism, this question is nonsense. Job and the major thinkers of the Hebrew tradition did not even *pretend* to understand. They would have appreciated and accepted Harlow Shapley's statement that the origin of origins is unknowable. Indeed, Shapley says, with proper scientific caution, that the origin of origins is *perhaps* unknowable. The ancient rabbinic

[4] Job 38:4, 7; 31, 33.
[5] Psalm 8:3–4.
[6] In *The Midrash on Psalms,* ed. William G. Broude (New Haven: Yale University Press, 1959), I, 275.

thinkers went much further. They asked that we accept the un-
knowability of ultimates. They enjoined us against speculation
on *"ma-aseh merkava,"* the mystical "chariot" of Ezekiel, and
"ma-aseh b'reshit," the work of creation. They told us that this
kind of speculation is "dangerous," that it can lead to superstition or, even worse, to madness and to death.[7]

Judaism, at its best, has always rested on wonder and humility, on what Abraham Joshua Heschel calls "radical amazement." The revelations of contemporary astrophysics serve but
to reinforce its prescientific intuitions. "He stretcheth out the
north over empty space and he hangeth the earth over nothing"
says Job, "Lo these are but the outskirts of His ways, and how
small a whisper is heard of Him! But the thunder of his mighty
deeds who can understand?" [8]

Harlow Shapley says we cannot understand the universe, because we are "dumb." We echo that word, in both its meanings.
We are dumb in the limitations on our organs of sense perception, we are dumb in the limitations on our intelligence, and we
are mute, before the wonders of our world. The more we recognize our limitations and the smaller we feel, the greater is the
wonder that is the root of our faith.

There is one very revealing speculation in the Talmud on the
thirteenth verse of Isaiah 14: "And thou hast said in thy heart,
I will ascend unto the stars, I will become like unto God." This
is the kind of presumption that both Shapley and high religion
would strike down. The mad space dreams of our day are in this
category. We have hardly ventured out of our own minuscule
planetary area, but we talk about space explorations and intergalactic travel. We think we are going to ascend "beyond the
heavens" and "become like God." The ancient sages tell us
that it was Nebuchadnezzar who presumed to say "I will ascend

[7] See Job 26:14, 42:3; cf. Deuteronomy 29:29. Talmud, Tractate
Chagigah, 14b (Soncino translation, pp. 90 ff.) and *Chagigah,* 11b:
"Whoever speculates on four things it would be better if he had never
been born: what is above, what is below, what before, what after" (Soncino, pp. 59 ff.).
[8] Job 26:7, 14.

into heaven . . . I will be like the Most High." [9] Of course, he was thrust down into the pit of ignorance. For, the sages calculate that the journey to the outermost ends of the heavens would take 7,500 years. The days of our years, they add, are threescore years and ten, or even by reason of strength fourscore years.[10]

You might say that these sages were "pikers." What is a 7,500-year journey—on muscle power alone at that—when we can talk about two billion light-years; two billion years at a speed of a 186,000 miles per second! But is there really any great difference, rhetorically speaking, between the position of man relative to a journey of 7,500 years and his position relative to one of two billion light-years?

A hoary anecdote tells of a man who was listening to a lecture by an outstanding scientist, and at one point in his lecture the scientist said, "In eighty billion years, the world will be destroyed!" The man jumped out of his seat and said, "What did you say? What did you say?" The lecturer answered, "I said that in eighty billion years the world will be destroyed." Our friend sat down and sighed, "What a relief! I thought you said *eighteen* billion years."

If then, reality is so incomprehensibly vast, so incalculably beyond us, how can we lay claim to a relationship with ultimate reality? This is the heart of the mystery. Those who find the word "God" "archaic," and who find any search for meaning or for a relationship with the universe unnecessary, will not be troubled by this question. But it is not unnecessary to hosts of thinking men, who need the assurance of ultimate meaning, of ultimate significance. And it is strange and magnificently reassuring that this stuff of which we are made is really one with the galaxies and with the stars.

It is not strange that there should be a relationship between us and the cosmos. We have learned that significance is not determined by size or by duration. Indeed, space and time are concepts that have been all but annihilated by modern physics. We know that one idea in one mind or even one physical event

[9] Isaiah 14:13, 14.
[10] Talmud, Tractate *Chagigah* 13a (Soncino, p. 74).

in one moment of time—for example, the primeval cooking of the heavier elements may have taken only an hour—one idea in one mind or one physical event may have greater significance than eons and eons of the slow circulation of one of the outer galaxies of stars.

Let me use an analogy of my own devising, which, though crude from a scientific standpoint, has frequently helped me with the problems of size and number. It helps me overcome the tendency to conclude that because I am so small in relation to the universe and but one among so incalculably many, I am therefore insignificant. This is my line of thought:

I contemplate my finger tip. I know that, in figurative and layman's terms, the number of atoms in that finger tip is "incalculable"—the figure would be astronomical. Nevertheless, every atom in my finger tip is, in an immediately recognizable sense, important to me. If one goes, so to speak, berserk, and a cell then goes berserk, as in cancerous tissue, I am in for trouble. Or if I neglectfully mash my finger in a door, the microscopic components of that finger tip may be said to be in for "trouble." Contemplating my finger tip, I am aware of the *relationship* between me and that atom. Yet the physical ratio of the size of that atom to the whole me is proportionately the same as the whole me is to the entire solar system out to Pluto and beyond!

I am not suggesting any Fechner-like organismic theory of the universe.[11] I am suggesting that in matters of relationship, size and quantity are *not* the most significant factors.[12]

In at least one area, however, the scientist and my faith are

[11] Gustav Theodor Fechner (1801–1887) believed that the universe displayed the characteristics of a living organism.

[12] A friend of mine at the Case Institute of Technology reinforces my argument with the following figures about the potentialities of a single human brain: the average human brain has 100,000,000,000,000 (10^{13}) cells. In order to write down the number of possible interconnections among those cells, a man writing 8 hours per day, 250 days per year, at a rate of 2 digits per second (not a bad rate for sustained writing) would be able to set down the entire figure in slightly less than 7,000,000 years. The figure itself (10 to the 100-trillionth power) is a sum larger than the number of electrons in the known universe!

in full agreement. The religionist has no dispensation to turn his gaze away from reality. Faith does not mean stubborn persistence in believing that which is absurd. Faith is persistence in the search for a structure of ultimate meaning that will support our ultimate concern.

Nothing that science has revealed lends credence to a view of the universe as capricious or absurd or as a result of "happenstance" or chance. Indeed, all that we learn from science supports the view that the universe is inherently and beautifully logical. That word "beautifully" is properly used. Einstein's pursuit of a unified field theory is one in which he engaged as much because of its aesthetic satisfaction as because of its mathematical and philosophical satisfaction.

Responding to such a universe, we could say with Harlow Shapley that "all we have to do is be good cosmic sports and play along with the game of growth." But that quip strikes me as far too flippant in the face of the overwhelming wonder that is the cosmos. It is a companion response to Shapley's gentlemanly acceptance of doom. When we do ourselves in, when we blow our world to smithereens, he says, it will not even be noticed by the stars.[13]

Now this judgment that the human episode is insignificant is a judgment of faith, not a scientific pronouncement. I cannot accept it.

Some would characterize this as anthropocentric overconcern. The end of the terrestrial human episode would not matter too much in the larger scheme of things. The death of individuals, the death of species, and even the death of worlds as an inevitable and ever present aspect of the unfoldment of cosmic evolution and death, does not connote absurdity. Indeed, the death of mankind may be the only possible meaningful denouement in the light of man's arrogance and spiritual inadequacy. "The end of all flesh is come before Me; for the earth is filled with violence through them; and, behold, I will destroy them with the earth." [14]

[13] "Stars, Ethics and Survival," in *Science Ponders Religion*, p. 12.
[14] Genesis 6:13.

Death, it is true, need not be equated with absurdity, but premature and unnecessary death is always tragedy. A premature end of the human episode must be judged to be tragedy. If there must be a "Day of Judgment," that day is cheapened and demeaned when it comes about through man's miscalculation. One cannot contemplate, without a sorrow beyond speech, the utter tragedy after the painful struggle of life through the ages to develop a being who is able to contemplate himself and to contemplate the cosmos, that the great spiritual potential of man should be wiped out by his collective stupidity and his collective inability to control his aggressions.

My faith tells me that there is spiritual significance in this human episode, whether it is short or long in duration, whether it is finite or infinite. It says that there is spiritual significance in the quest of the men of science themselves, in the pioneering spirits who are pushing back the frontiers of knowledge, in the quest for truth, in the gallant stand of tiny man. There is spiritual significance in our effort to penetrate the secrets of the universe in order to learn how we are related to ultimate reality. There are, however, other modes of relating ourselves to that reality, and to these we now turn.

CHAPTER EIGHT

TO WHOM DO WE PRAY?

If we want to bring into focus the problems that agitate the radical theologians, we have only to raise the problem of prayer. For one thing, most religions—whatever else they may or may not do—prescribe some kind of discipline of prayer.[1] For another, most prayer is intended to be a form of communication. It is addressed to someone or something. We beg the question, of course, when we ask "To Whom Do We Pray?" Prayer may be viewed as an exercise in introspection, as meditation—which it often is—requiring no Object. Or it may be viewed as an exercise in relationship, in which case a reality that is the other pole of that relationship is required, unless we respond to Nothingness. This last is exactly what we do, according to many radical theologians. Not that they have as yet adequately considered the effect of the new theology on the disciplines of religion. Nor have they dealt with the question of prayer. It may well be dead for them and the question obsolete.

Richard Rubenstein, a rabbi who identifies himself with the "death-of-God" theologians, tells us that we are responding to that Nothingness out of which we came and into which we shall go. He writes: "When I say we live in a time of the death of God, I mean that the thread uniting God and man, heaven and earth has been broken. We stand in a cold, silent, unfeeling cosmos, unaided by any purposeful power beyond our own resources. After Auschwitz, what else can a Jew say about God?"

[1] See Friedrich Heiler, *Prayer* (New York: Oxford University Press, 1932), p. xiii.

And further, "in the final analysis, omnipotent Nothingness is Lord of all creation." [2]

If God has no relevance to our world, or if the idea of God is irrelevant, it makes no sense to address Him at all. If God permitted Auschwitz to occur, it is craven gesture to petition Him for any human good at all. The problem of Auschwitz overwhelms every sensitive human being, and to every Jew it is agonizing. Its obscene depravity mocks the Divine. But Auschwitz introduces no new problems: it is the old problem of evil written large; [3] it differs only quantitatively from prior problems. Every time a single righteous person is cut off in youth, it is an Auschwitz; every time an innocent individual suffers, it is an Auschwitz; every time a Negro is brutally beaten to death, it is an Auschwitz. It does not require 6,000,000 deaths to evoke a picture of absurdity, injustice, or of the depths of wickedness to which men may sink.

But the very word "prayer" means "petition," and petitional prayer is awkward for modern man for reasons other than the problem of evil. It is a dead-end hangover from those ritual

[2] In a symposium, *Commentary*, XLII, 2 (August 1966), pp. 134 ff. See also *After Auschwitz: Radical Theology and Contemporary Judaism* (New York: The Bobbs-Merrill Company, Inc., 1966), pp. 230 ff. Here he defines what he has called "the Holy Nothingness" in terms of that view of the "primordial Godhead" that is present in Jewish mysticism.

"Nothingness," as used by Rubenstein, is a theological term. Like the mystics, he ascribes qualities to it, such as "a certain fullness." It is, therefore, also a metaphorical way of speaking. Cyril Richardson is apt and insightful here when, speaking about what he calls "the Infinites," he says:

If we talk at all it is in images, analogies which point only to the mysteries which confront us and which we cannot grasp . . . three are basic. We can call the Infinites "the gods," attributing to them positive being and some characteristics of personality. Here the images evoked provide the ultimate security and cleansing of self. We can call the Infinites "the universe." Here the images evoked offer the embrace of of the womb, the warmth of being united again with the "isness" of life . . . Finally we can call the Infinites "the nothingness." Here the images call us to final resignation and to acceptance of the meaninglessness of existence. Here the death wish conquers. (Cyril Richardson, "Do the Gods Exist?" in *Religious Experience and Truth*, ed. Sidney Hook [New York: New York University Press, 1961], p. 286).

[3] See below, Chapter XI, for a fuller discussion of this.

practices of religion that were intended to manipulate the world—to bring rain, or avert cyclones, or make the fields yield a rich harvest. It is akin to that magic that once had a shady and disreputable association with religion but that is really the primitive forerunner of science, both of the laboratory and of contemporary technology. It survives in the kind of religion that seeks to make God into a "gimmick," to use him as a "cosmic bellhop," to exploit a relationship with him as a means of achieving popularity, getting rich or achieving "Success," the undefined bitch-goddess of the Western world. In Buber's terms, of which more later, this is the effort to make an "It" of "the Thou that cannot become It."

The attempt to make prayer an instrument—in other words, the use of prayer as a form of magic—although it has no intellectual approval, is a tenaciously held aspect of much present-day religion. That this is the realm of science rather than religion—good or bad science or magic-science, but nevertheless science—is dramatized by the advertising campaign carried on not too long ago in behalf of a book called *The Power of Prayer on Plants,* by Dr. Franklin Loehr. This book was touted as offering "scientific proof of the power of prayer over life and death," as the result of "900 controlled laboratory experiments"! The advertisement was illustrated by a photograph, which showed that seeds that had been "prayed over" grew more rapidly than those that had not received the benefit of such attention.

The intellectual is scornful of such claims, as he is scornful of the parapsychology laboratories at Duke University. But scorn is an inadequate response to that which adopts the scientific laboratory method. What is called for is a critical analysis of the laboratory techniques used, and either verification or refutation of the announced results.

Much of what the popular mind associates with religion—necromancy, magic, soothsaying, incantations—is that aspect of ancient thought and practice that has given way in the modern world to scientific method. It is immature and impatient science—the attempt through formulas or prescribed actions to manipulate the physical world, or the belief that certain causes (such as walking under a ladder) have invariable, predictable effects. This part of the complex of man's response to the world has been separated out of mature religion by mature science.

This is not wholly modern: overt and recognizable superstition (literally, "religious practice founded on fear or ignorance") was frowned upon by Biblical Judaism and proscribed through the ages in traditional Judaism up to the modern prayer of the contemporary Reform Jew in his Union Prayer Book: "May the time not be distant . . . when superstition shall no longer enslave the mind." [4] Long before the cult was cleansed of practices we would label superstitious, one of the earliest of Jewish codes enjoined the people of Israel against practicing augury and witchcraft or turning to "ghosts" or "familiar spirits" or to charmers and necromancers "who consult the dead," [5] practices that were common to the peoples with whom they were surrounded. "After the doings of the land of Egypt, wherein ye dwelt, shall ye not do: and after the doings of the land of Canaan, whither I bring you, shall ye not do. . . ." [6] Rabbinic tradition ascribes to a great third-century teacher who lived in Babylon and whose name was Mar Samuel, the saying *"Ayn mazal l'yisrael"*—popularly interpreted, "Jews have no luck," but really enjoining Jews against ascribing potency to "mazal," the practice of astrology—looking for lucky and unlucky omens in the stars in their zodiacal divisions.[7]

It must be admitted that folk religion constantly breaks through these insights, and even in the passages we have cited a veiled respect for unseen forces and influences may be discerned. In the customs and practices that ordinary people have associated with religion, superstition has been rampant. It is also pervasive among the supposedly sophisticated moderns of our "enlightened" twentieth century. In many large buildings,

---

[4] In the prayer known as the *Alenu* in the *Union Prayer Book* (Cincinnati: Central Conference of American Rabbis, 1947), I, 71, and elsewhere. The Hebrew original speaks of the elimination of *gilulim* and *elilim:* "false gods" and "idols."

[5] Leviticus 19:31; Deuteronomy 18:9 ff.

[6] Leviticus 18:3.

[7] Talmud, Tractate *Sabbath* 156 a-b (Soncino translation, p. 800).

the thirteenth floor does not exist. The number 13 is avoided by people who never knew that Jesus had twelve disciples and that the superstition attached to the number 13 arises out of the story of the Last Supper. Some Jews knock on wood without knowing that they are evoking thereby the "saving image of the Cross," and people avoid black cats without any conscious belief that the cats might be familiar spirits or witches in disguise, which is the origin of distrust of black cats.

A probably apocryphal tale is told about the great Talmudist, my teacher, the late Dr. Jacob Lauterbach at the Hebrew Union College in Cincinnati. Dr. Lauterbach was an inveterate exposer of the superstitious origins of many our rituals and customs, and he used to inveigh in the classroom against taking seriously *mazikin,* "injurious spirits," or *shaydim,* "evil spirits or demons." One night he was taking his usual postprandial stroll. Dr. Lauterbach was a great eater, and he was walking up and down outside the dormitory letting his dinner settle. Suddenly, some of the students noticed that he had stopped in his tracks. In the shrubbery, next to the walk, there was a little black cat. Dr. Lauterbach stood there and said, "Go 'way, cat, go 'way cat." The students clustered around and said, "Dr. Lauterbach, don't tell us you're afraid of a black cat, don't tell us that you believe in that superstition." Dr. Lauterbach answered, "I don't believe in it . . . but why take chances?"

Dr. Lauterbach was unconsciously quoting the *Sefer Chasidim,* a medieval work in which Y'hudah ben Sh'muel of Regensburg says, with a straight face, "One should not believe in superstition, but it is best to be heedful of them." In other words, "Why take chances?".

Actually, they were not altogether wrong. One of the popular superstitions, for example, was that one does not leave food uncovered overnight because if one leaves it so, the demons will enter into it. This sounds persuasive, as anyone who has had ptomaine poisoning would know.

Superstition is not, however, "religion" in any contemporary mature understanding of the term. It is rather an attempt to find techniques that will produce certain pragmatic results. Religion's role here should be evaluative, rather than functional.

It is interesting to note in this connection that the Talmud [8] distinguishes among and evaluates three different forms of magic. There is, first, the magic that attempts to change reality by means of witchcraft, incantations, and spells. This is not only forbidden, but it is theoretically punishable by stoning ("theoretically," for the death penalty was never applied in post-Biblical times). The second form of magic is the magic of illusion: "now you see it, now you don't," the magic of the entertainment stage. This, too, is forbidden by the rabbis, but because it is relatively harmless no penalty is attached to it as such. (Of course, any attempt to defraud or exploit, using such means, would be punishable.) The third form of magic is that which takes place when dedicated men work with the laws of creation to produce specific and tangible results—and this is permitted *ab initio*. In the Talmud, this last form is illustrated by the legend of two rabbis who through work and study were able to create a third-grown calf, on which they then dined; by extension and by analogy, it means the kind of scientific endeavor that explores the frontiers of the physical order both in the macrocosm and in the microcosm, and that gives us the technological miracles of our time.

Institutional religion, as well as folk religion, has frequently yielded to superstitious practices by rationalizing or sublimating them. Many of the Jewish customs that we take for granted are sublimated forms of superstition. The breaking of the glass at a Jewish wedding was originally an effort to frighten away the night demons, and especially Lilith, by throwing the glass against the north wall of the courtyard. It has been reinterpreted as a *zecher l'churbon,* a reminder of the destruction of the Temple, the moment of sadness in the midst of joy. The covering of mirrors in the home of the bereaved is rationalized today by saying that we do not want the mourners to see their own tear-stricken visages. But this was done originally because a reflection was believed to be a projection of the soul, and the demons hovering

[8] Tractate *Sanhedrin* 67b (Soncino translation, pp. 459 ff.).

about might carry off the soul of the living! The custom of washing the hands on returning from the cemetery was intended to rid oneself of the demons that follow one back from the cemetery and that cluster about one.

Indeed, how many superstitions seem to bear the endorsement of religious tradition: The *komayah* that a child and frequently an adult would wear about his neck bearing the name of God, or bearing *abracadabra,* in its original sense (*Abraych davro*—"may the word disappear"—taking the demon's name and allowing it to disappear in words broken down into syllables and finally into letters and then nothingness), or the changing of names to change fortune; or the fear of the word that would invite the envy of evil spirits. "What a beautiful baby, *unbeschrien! unberufen! absit omen, k'nayinhora!* May the evil eye be averted!" To say it is a beautiful baby is to invite its destruction or its later ugliness, and so a phrase must be added to propitiate the evil spirits.

Let me illustrate this entanglement by referring to a latter-day practice that has grown up with the tacit endorsement of supposed religious functionaries. It is the obligation of a pious son in the first eleven months of bereavement to join a *minyan,* a quorum for prayer, daily, to say the *Kaddish,* Judaism's preeminent hymn of praise to God, as an act of filial piety to his deceased father. I found out recently and quite to my amazement that the son who does not "have time" to recite *Kaddish* for his father may, in any one of three or four synagogues in my city, be able to *purchase* a *Kaddish,* to pay a minyan-man to say the *Kaddish* for him while he sleeps a bit later or goes down to work earlier every morning! This is abracadabra, the empty ritual form spoken by someone else, founded on fear and on ignorance.

I have been deeply troubled by those who will say to me, in all sincerity, "Rabbi, pray for me," or more frequently, "Rabbi, pray for *him.*" How can one say "no"? One may attempt gently to instruct by saying, "Of course I'll pray, but the most important praying is the praying that you'll do yourself." And yet even as I say that, it violates every deep conviction that I hold with regard to the role of prayer. Prayer in Judaism, at its best, is not a device to effect changes in the world—to bring about revisions in the material world—nor is prayer an instrument for tangible objectives. Prayer is a search for meaning. It is an expression of aspiration, a venture into relationship. It is not a bid for favors, and it is certainly not a charm or a magic formula. The praying individual must be *present*. Present in more than one sense: present in relationship to the eternal Thou, present spiritually as well as present physically.

This applies to our discussion of petitional prayer. If petitional prayer is only a cry of distress into the Void, a dramatic expression of human need without expectation of an answer, it may serve some psychologically demonstrable therapeutic purpose, but it is not petition in any meaningful use of the word. It is a ritual, designed as are all rituals, according to a psychologist friend of mine, "to get rid of the accumulated crud." This is a useful process, but hardly an exalted one. It makes of religion a kind of purgative, which should endear it to all who seek new functional foundations for religion.

Prayer, however, has frequently been, and as frequently is, something other than crass petition and something other than talking to oneself. Prayer in its finest moment is a *confrontation*—the effort to stand in relationship to that which is ultimate, to all that is antithetical to triviality, fragmentation, expediency, transiency, and to find that which is enduring and that which is most important. It is an expression of that "will to meaning" of which we have already spoken, and it is a necessary exercise of that will. This is the mood of the kind of prayer that is reflected in the Psalmist's cry: "As the hart panteth after the water brooks, So panteth my soul after Thee, O God. My soul thirsteth for God, for the living God . . ." [9] What the Psalmist seeks here is the sense of God's *presence*, the assurance that his melancholy, "cast-down" mood is not final, that absurdity and evil need not triumph. Prayer here is more the quest for conviction than it is the affirmation of conviction. The Psalmist "waits" for God as the assurance that there is that which is more endur-

[9] Psalm 42:1–2.

ing than men, who when set in the balance are as "nothingness." Yet that very transiency of man can be a challenge to him to make the most of his situation, if he can but learn to "number" his days in order to achieve wisdom.[10] In this type of prayer, the Psalmist verbalizes the central existential problem of man, even as he affirms that in spite of everything, there is meaning.

The Psalmist also confronts God as the source of Ultimate Demand, the guarantor of his ethical values. His prayer then becomes a plea for instruction, for guidance, and for even stronger demands upon him. "Teach me Thy way" is his reiterated plea, "that I may walk in Thy truth"; "Send forth Thy light and Thy truth, let them lead me"; "Make me to tread in the path of thy commandments (*mitzvah*)." [11]

The feeling that the Psalmist in his prayer stands in full relationship, that he is engaged in a dialogue, is strengthened by his assumption of the right to reverse the process and make demands upon the universe. There is a Promethean element in the Psalms as there is in Job and in Jeremiah. "Why standest Thou afar off, O Lord?" he cries. "Why hidest Thou Thyself in times of trouble?" Or more insistently—and in the light of the horrors of our time, poignantly—he calls God to account: "Yea, but for Thy sake are we killed all the day; We are accounted as sheep for the slaughter. Awake, why sleepest Thou, O Lord? Wherefore hidest Thou Thy face, and forgettest our affliction and our oppression?" [12]

We feel justified in drawing thus heavily on the Hebrew Psalms because the Psalter is the major thesaurus of Western prayer, reflecting all its moods and defining its normative form. We may not be able to feel "after Auschwitz"—and my own sense of my relationship to God awakens in me no need to feel it—that God is a source of comfort, an ever-present help in trouble, a Shepherd who provides all our wants. But when the Psalmist seeks the Source of meaning and stands before the Source of demand, it is possible to empathize into his prayer

[10] See Psalms 62 and 90.
[11] Psalms 27:11; 86:11; 43:3; 119:35.
[12] Psalms 10:1; 44:22–24.

and even to find in him a treasury of presently meaninful prayer language.

This is why the Psalms provide the mainstay of public worship for both Jews and Christians. Because corporate prayer is the public expression of shared values, hopes and needs, the Psalter provides an anthology of rhetorical gems in which the whole gamut of such hopes, values, and needs finds expression.

But public worship is a special problem. A worship "service" is a complex exercise, in which the community, in the sense of a group that does possess shared values, or the recognition of shared destiny or need, seeks both confrontation and the expression of those central values, aspirations, and responsibilities. Its difficulties stem from its tendency to become liturgical, and thus conservative in the retention of specific forms, specific language, and traditional terms of speech and address. Much of what fixed liturgy puts in our mouths is jagged and awkward if it passes through our minds.

This has been my experience in dealing with the prayer literature of my own branch of American Judaism. The traditional Jewish prayer book—the *Siddur*—has been called an encyclopedia of Judaism. In the cumulative devotions and supplications, prayers and study passages that have grown up within the synagogue, in the *Siddur* in its pristine form, we see reflected the experience of the Jewish people, especially the experience of our 2,000 years of dispersion, the period in which this prayer book came into being. The Union Prayer Book used by Reform Jews is an attenuated version of the *Siddur*. It has excised a great deal of that historic trek and of its end products in poetry, in thought, and in prayer. Indeed, the Union Prayer Book is a response to the mood of a specific age. It began to take shape in the late nineteenth century, and although it has gone through three revisions it has not changed very much. The general tenor of its formulations and selections reflects the optimism that marked the thinking of men at the turn of the century. Those Hebrew passages that are retained are, even for those who understand them, not too difficult to take. Some of its flights of

English paraphrase and addition are, however, at this point in our spiritual development, positively embarrassing.

We read, for example, in the free rendition of a prayer praising wondrous deliverances in Jewish history:

> . . . through Thy power alone has Israel been redeemed from the hand of oppressors . . .
> Thou hast kept us in life; Thou hast not let our footsteps falter.
> Thy love has watched over us in the night of oppression;
> Thy mercy has sustained us in the hour of trial.
> And now that we live in a land of freedom, may we continue to be faithful to Thee and Thy word.[13]

Anyone who is responsive to the mood of contemporary Jewish history, who has an iota of understanding of the meaning of the Holocaust, of what our people have been through, must read this passage with a feeling of shame. To say "Thy mercy has sustained us in the hour of trial," or "Thy love has watched over us in the night of oppression," after 6,000,000 have gone to the gas chambers, to the crematories, and to cruel mass deaths, after the long years of suffering and exile have come to this incredible climax, is a sickening blasphemy. This is not the mood of our prayer today. Our mood must be the mood of search, the effort to understand how the bestiality of man could reach such depths. Nor is it the mood of the *Siddur,* the traditional prayer book. For what the Union Prayer Book did was to take the sense of security that the Jews of the late nineteenth century felt in America and translate it into a permanent sense of safety and security, cutting out of the prayer book all references to exile or to suffering, presenting the world as "all sweetness and light."

As the content of man's experience is constantly changing in response to historical development and in even new and often unprecedented situations, so the content of what man brings to his relationship with God must be ever different. His expectations change, his needs change, his mood changes, but it is possible to affirm that what he confronts is in its ultimacy and impene-

[13] *Union Prayer Book,* I, 16.

trability unchanged. His understanding of the demand made upon him may be false, partial, or inadequate; but his posture of openness and of need is, in its deep humanity, one that links him with his earliest forebears.

Through all the changes, when man stands in prayer, his relationship is, and essentially must be, "personal." Whether he addresses God as "Lord" or as "Father" or "Great Spirit" or "Master of the Universe," or whether he apostrophizes the "Source of all meaning and all truth," or whether he says only "Thou," his posture if he prays at all is inevitably grounded in the limitations of the constructs produced by the human mind and accessible to human experience. He is inescapably anthropomorphic. He even at times and in certain periods of development falls into an intimacy that reflects his family relationships. The way in which Sholom Aleichem's Tevye talks to God is a realistic portrayal of an aspect of East European Jewish folk culture. The East European Jew—in all his pre-Hitlerian misery— found it possible to address God as *Tatenyu:* an untranslatable Yiddish diminutive term of endearment for "Father," perhaps akin to "Daddy" (the shocking ridiculousness and childishness of the English word in such a context is not present in the Yiddish vocative, which is redeemed by its utter sincerity). Even a term such as *boray olam,* "creator of the universe," is invested with personal intimacy by this culture. This is illustrated in an anecdote, which Franz Rosenzweig tells about Hermann Cohen, the great Neo-Kantian thinker associated with the so-called "Marburg" school of thought. Cohen taught at the University of Marburg, and while there "he once expounded the God-idea of his *Ethics* to an old Jew of that city. The Jew listened with reverent attention, but when Cohen was through, he asked: 'And where is the *boray olam?*' Cohen had no answer to this, and tears rose in his eyes." [14]

It is in connection with this anecdote that Rosenzweig points out that the immanence-transcendence dichotomy—which we have tried to avoid in speaking of all-that-is—never had reality

[14] Nahum N. Glatzer, *Franz Rosenzweig: His Life and Thought* (Philadelphia: Jewish Publication Society, 1953), p. 282.

in the thought-life of the pious Jew. Once again, in life "as it is lived," *both* ends of the paradox are affirmed. Commenting on a couplet of Judah Halevi, the eleventh-century poet and philosopher, Rosenzweig writes:

> Here *boray olam* . . . does not mean something remote, as the content of the words seems to indicate. On the contrary: in popular speech the words are fraught with emotion, they are something near, and in the case of the God of the heart, the heart never for a moment forgets that He is the one—who *is*. So here the spark does not merely oscillate between the two poles of nearness and remoteness, but each pole itself has a positive and negative charge, only in different pattern. The Creator who is above the world takes up his "habitation," and the abstract God of philosophy has his "being" in the crushed heart.[15]

The *boray olam* of the immediate Jewish past, the intimately known and tenderly beloved Father of the Universe, is not present in most contemporary theologizing and, like Hermann Cohen, we may well weep for His absence. Indeed, the religious naturalists disparage this response to God as a response to a "cosmic papa." They feel that as "moderns" enamored of that same empiricism belatedly exalted by the "death-of-God" thinkers, they speak with greater integrity and with greater faithfulness to reason when they use the term "process." We agree that our universe appears to us as a universe of order and coherence. We want to utilize our reason to its uttermost limits. We reject magic and the superstitious use of prayer. We understand that prayer is not intended to manipulate God. But because we do not believe—in William James's phrase—that God is a "cosmic bellhop," that we have but to push the button and he will dance to our request, is it necessary that we think of God as "process" or "energy" or "force"? This insistence that God is "cosmic process" and not "cosmic person" troubles me. It suggests a kind of certainty about the nature of God and a diminished recognition of the profundity of our limitations.

I know when I address God as person that I am using a meta-

[15] Glatzer, p. 282.

phor, I am substituting a poetic expression concerning something that I can describe for that which is beyond description. When I say "Thou," to God, when I say "God is my Father" and "God is the Father of all mankind," I am making use of terms accessible to me to express an experience of relationship that I can adequately articulate only in "soft-focus" language. When the empirical naturalists speak of a "cosmic process," do they recognize with equal conviction that they, too, are using a metaphor?

Contemporary physics uses these terms with much greater exactitude and with a certain wariness. Many accepted constituents of the physical universe are "constructs" projected from the "plane of experience," where only their effects may be studied,[16] and even these effects are distorted by the act of investigation, as the "uncertainty principle" of Werner Heisenberg and Niels Bohr tells us. Indeed, we learn things about the "onta," particles of inanimate nature such as the electron, that defy common sense and suggest comparison with abstract qualities like love that are subject to Alfred North Whitehead's "fallacy of simple location," in that they are real "and yet do not permit description" in terms of position or quantity; they defy visualization; and they lead to such speculations as Bohr's concept of complementarity, "the need for dual types of description of human experience, as inevitable, as grounded in the nature of things and in the limitations of man's understanding." [17]

Even scientists are subject to the need to "express" what they learn verbally as well as in mathematical formulas, and so they, too, have recourse to metaphor, talking in terms of human sense perception and using the language of "waves" and "particles." It does no harm, says Henry Margenau, "if the physicist tries to explain the erratic behavior of the atomic world by a reference to causative agencies; it affords him comfort and makes the microcosm seem less strange." [18]

[16] See Henry Margenau, *Open Vistas* (New Haven: Yale University Press, 1961), p. 181.
[17] Margenau, pp. 161 ff.
[18] Margenau, p. 139.

The religionist who says "cosmic process" instead of "cosmic person" and believes he has thereby advanced in rationality should also know that he is being anthropomorphic and using a term that describes a sequentiality or unfolding that is accessible to us in the restricted observation point we occupy as human beings. A leading astrophysicist, who through most of his professional career was associated with the Mount Wilson Observatory, Gustaf Stromberg, put it this way:

> Fields of force, radiation, waves and particles are *constructs of the human mind.* They are invented by ingenious story tellers to describe and explain the observed shadow play; in pictorial form for most of us, in mathematical form for people interested in quantitative research and in practical applications, and in more abstruse terms for the philosophically minded. Like all allegories, the stories are expressed in terms and symbols appropriate to the understanding of the people to whom they are presented . . .[19]

The metaphors used by both science and religion must neither belie experience nor outrage reason. They must enhance the verbal communication of that experience in those areas where steno-language is inadequate. I do not know that this enhancement is achieved when we substitute a metaphor like "process" for a metaphor like "person." Indeed, something is lost—for "process" does not enhance our effort to describe the experience of relationship. It neither belies my experience nor outrages reason for me, when I say that I feel in prayer a sense of direct relationship to all-that-is and I describe that relationship as "personal."

All relationship is, of course, a two-way affair. "Let no attempt be made to sap the strength from the meaning of the relation: relation is mutual," says Martin Buber, in a context in which it is difficult to make a sense model of that mutuality.[20] This reciprocal character inherent in relationship is made evi-

[19] In his essay, "The Physical and the Non-Physical Worlds," which appears as an appendix to his book *The Soul of the Universe* (Philadelphia: De Vorss, 1940), pp. 243 f.

[20] Martin Buber, *I and Thou,* 2nd ed. (New York: Charles Scribner's Sons, 1958), p. 8; he is referring to an I-Thou relationship with a tree.

dent in popular speech when someone says, "I cannot relate to him. I have tried again and again, but he is cold and unresponsive. He doesn't seem to know I'm there." To "relate" is to be open to the other in all his complexity and all his need. To relate is to "turn toward." There is no relationship when one is turned inward. "You know, Bill," said a friend of mine to a mutual acquaintance who was reputed to be abnormally and invariably self-centered, and whom he was deliberately testing, "I was in Denver last week for a physical examination and they told me I had cancer." "Is that so?" said Bill. "I spoke in Denver last year."

Usually, when we say "I cannot relate to him," we are making a negative judgment about the other person. But if relationship is openness to the total complexity of the other, it is possible to be wholly present even to the naive and unconscious self-absorption of a Bill. What we usually mean, however, is a situation in which there is no response, no feeling of *any kind* of reciprocal communication. There is no escaping that having a sense of relationship to God must mean having a sense of communication. At the very least, it must mean that our responding to God indicates that we are open to the divine address, and a fulfilled sense of relationship must include a sense of being addressed. This is where the traditional inarticulateness of religious experience becomes most evident and where the affirmation of both sides of the transcendent-immanent, unknowable-intimately-known paradox frustrates all those who look for an exact semantic or who wish to submit to analysis propositional statements by those who claim such experience. Both the ambivalence and the affirmation of relationship is found in Judah Halevi's lyrical echo of the Psalms:

> Lord, where shall I find Thee?
> High and hidden is Thy place;
> And where shall I not find Thee?
> The world is full of Thy glory.

. . . .

I have sought Thy nearness
With all my heart have called Thee,
And going out to meet Thee
I found Thee coming toward me . . .[21]

When we stand in relationship, responding to all-that-is and sensing or feeling its response to us, we cannot help but react in personal terms. This is so, even though the ultimate reality to which we open ourselves is beyond our comprehension. We verbalize about love, compassion, sympathy, or justice—all are human emotions or human value-terms. Many of the naturalist religious thinkers prefer to speak of God as "intelligence." But "intelligence" is no less a human characteristic than "compassion." If it is possible to conceive of God as "cosmic intelligence," why is it not equally possible to conceive of him as cosmic love, cosmic sympathy, and cosmic justice?

We know that if we are permitted to use such terms about God at all, we are really using human feeling-states only as an analogy. The love and justice of God must, by definition, be the human responses sublimated to their nth degree. The affirmation that love and justice are written into the very structure of the universe—that they are attributes of the Divine—is a statement of intuition, an extrapolation of experience, or a leap of faith. The belief that cosmic evolution is laboring in the direction of greater harmony, greater coherence, and ever-more-refined consciousness is also an extrapolation from the known to the unknown. Hatred, injustice, ugliness, and ignorance are realities against which all-that-is moves, and we are called to ally ourselves with all-that-is in the struggle. Incoherence, disharmony, conflict, and matter devoid of consciousness are the raw evils against which cosmic evolution labors. It does not outrage reason to believe that man is able to respond to its call.

Such a response becomes real only in action. But the prayer that says "Teach me Thy will," or "Help me to respond to others in that love which I find in Thee," is preparatory to action. It

[21] Judah Halevi, *Selected Poems,* trans. Nina Saloman (Philadelphia: Jewish Publication Society, 1928), pp. 134–135.

is petitional prayer but certainly worlds away from the manipulative petition that says, "God help me to become vice-president in charge of sales" or "Bring rain, O Lord." Any prayer that expects a departure from the order of the universe or an intervention in the world of experience is immature prayer. The universe just does not work that way. But I satisfy a deep need—as valid as that which lies behind my hunger for love, or for art, or for music, or for knowledge—when I stand before the experienced reality I address as God, and cry "Give me strength" or "Give me wisdom" or "Help me!"

We have not explained anything in doing this, nor have we performed any operational function. We have but exposed our limitations to the universe and sought within them to fulfill our potentialities. How could we carry on such an enterprise without caricaturing it, in any mood but that of deep humility? With Job, we must repeat, "Lo, these are but the outskirts of His ways, and how small a whisper is heard of him! But the thunder of his mighty deeds who can understand?" [22]

We have but an intuition of relationship. When we stand in prayer we experience it as we experience relationship to all men and to all life everywhere in the vastness of a universe whose outer reaches, the scientists tell us, are beyond the capacity of men to know them, possibly forever.

What we experience is Presence: the presence of that which endows life with significance and which sets its goals. And we may, without apology, call that Presence "Father" and "King" and "Lord of All."

[22] Job 26:14.

PART THREE

A RESPONSE FOR OUR TIME

But Thou art God who lives and endures . . .
. . . V-ata hu melech el chai v'kayam!
from the prayer N'taneh tokef,
recited on the Jewish High Holydays

CHAPTER NINE

THE SENSE OF PRESENCE

When we use the word "God," we testify to an aspect of our experience. When we stand in prayer, we seek to give expression to the feelings that accompany that experience. Among other emotions, we feel our creaturehood and dependence and so we frequently fall into the petitional mood. Since we suggested in the preceding chapter that petition is inutile except in the cathartic or dynamic effect it has on the praying individual, what then is the use of the relationship we are affirming?

This is a question which is made inevitable by the functional stance of modern man. Does it "do any good" to stand in relationship to all-that-is, either for the Whole that is the other pole of the relationship, or for the human beings who affirm the reality of that to which they turn?

Surely this is not the controlling question. Some things are good or true or compelling in themselves apart from any consideration of their functional aspects. Of what "use" is it to respond to the power of a symphony or to the breath-stopping beauty of a special sunset?

Function is allied to purpose, however. To deny purposiveness to the universe is to fall into the ambit of the philosophies of absurdity. I am not, therefore, ready to abandon the effort to establish the "value" or the "usefulness" of what we affirm when we speak of God.

In the chapters that follow, I shall seek to establish both the reality and the effect of the relationship. How do we "experience" it and what demand does it make upon us?

The word "demand" will grow increasingly important in the

pages yet to come and will in some degree respond to the question of utility. If there are "demands" which are aspects of ultimate reality, then there must be value in the fulfillment of such demands, both for the source of demand and for that upon which the demand is made.

Since the nature of a relationship may be fruitfully examined in the historic experience of a group that has affirmed it, I want first to attempt to examine one aspect of that relationship as it was given expression in the thought-life of the Jewish people. We have already argued that value-terms are more than "mere" words, that they are symbols which record, preserve, and transmit the multiple facets of experience. We can in great part learn what the Divine Presence has been in the experience of the Jew by a careful analysis of the evolutionary development of the verbal expression that has been given to that sense of presence.

The phrase, "sense of presence," evokes associations with mysticism and supernaturalism that obscure its significance. Actually, it seeks to describe an experience. It deals with a response to which men have testified and which they have sought to label and describe through the centuries. In the South Pacific, it was called *mana;* among American Indians, it was *orenda* or *wakan* or *manitu.* Sometimes, it was a sense of a power great enough to be dangerous, calling into being the associated idea of *tabu.* Sometimes, it was a sense of creature-feeling and reverence—a *mysterium tremendum*—for which Rudolf Otto coined the word "numinous." [1] Even as committed a religious naturalist as Mordecai Kaplan speaks of "God felt as presence," telling us that "God must not merely be held as an idea" and that "the actual awareness of His presence" is "experienced as beatitude and inner illumination." [2]

These responses betray a realistic meeting with the fact that in all our experiences there is more than can be comprehended by the human senses with their admitted limitations. The fact

[1] Rudolf Otto, *The Idea of the Holy,* trans. John W. Harvey (London: Oxford University Press, 1923).
[2] Mordecai M. Kaplan, *The Meaning of God in Modern Jewish Religion* (New York: Behrman House, Inc., 1937), p. 244.

that this "more" eludes those senses makes it neither unnatural nor supernatural. However, it is a "more" that demands respect and that rewards openness and receptivity to its address. The reward is enriched appreciation of that which we confront—fellow human beings or phenomena of nature—and an enriched appreciation of all-that-is.

This "sense of presence" is both a major characteristic and a primary motivation in Judaism. The chief carrier of the concept and the term most frequently used to point to the reality that it strives to apprehend is *kadosh,*[3] usually and inadequately translated as "holy," and the derivative concepts of *kiddush hashem* and *kiddush hachaim:* that is, making the divine presence manifest through human action and infusing life with the divine presence. This is the primary vocation of man, according to Jewish thought: to insure that presence *in the world* and in human relationships. Those who are looking for a "new language" and a "new style" adequate to the this-worldly demands of our age would do well to take a closer look at this idea of *kedushah.*[4]

An understanding of the way in which the term *kadosh* and its derivatives function in Jewish thought must be based on an effort to see the word in the multiple contexts of its total historical development and use. Words like these, as we have already tried to demonstrate, are not simply designative signs. They provide that "background of closely woven multiple meanings against which all conscious experiences and interpretations are measured."[5] Because such words are, in Philip Wheelwright's term, "multisignitive," they cannot be easily translated.

Kadosh is definitely not "holy." The word's meaning, like that of other central value-terms, is not fully communicated by

[3] A more specialized term is *Shechinah,* a word first used by the Targumim (Aramaic translations of Scripture) and by the rabbis to signify "the Presence of God."

[4] The abstract noun-form for *kadosh. Kadosh* is either an adjective or, with the definite article, the specific designation for the Presence.

[5] Susanne K. Langer, *Philosophy in a New Key: A Study in the Symbolism of Reason, Rite, and Art* (Cambridge, Mass.: Harvard University Press, 1942), p. 285.

most contemporary interpreters, because they yield to the temptation to *translate* rather than to *feel* the word with all its layers of charged meaning in its varied settings. The English word "holy" is the charged symbol of another tradition: primarily, the tradition of Anglo-Saxon Protestantism that gives it such associations as "separation," "quiet," "churchly things," "Gothic arches," and "praying hands."

Because such words become the foci of hosts of associations and of developing and shifting concepts of central significance in the cultures out of which they come, I call them "cluster-words." *Kadosh* is the most important cluster-word in Judaism and, properly understood, provides the key to the Jewish value-stance and the Jewish approach to relationship. To that end, it should be examined in its many successive layers of growth, all to be found in the fully developed concept. Nothing of the history of the word is lost, and this gives it the character of being "charged"—with propulsive content.

All the earliest associations of the word *kadosh* point to its close kinship with the Melanesian-Polynesian word *mana,* to which we have already alluded. It was an awesome and even lethal power that inhered in persons and objects, in groves and pillars and specially designated chests. Such objects could be approached only by those vested with the proper authority and in appropriate circumstances.[6]

There was nothing moral or rational about this. "Do not touch, lest you die" was a statement of sombre "fact," like a sign on a high-voltage power line. This is illustrated in the story of Uzzah, when David was bringing the Ark back from the Philistines. When they reached the threshing-floor of Nachon, the oxen stumbled. Uzzah saw the Ark about to slip from the cart and with a most natural gesture of reverent concern, he put out his hand to steady it. Contact was enough; he was immediately struck dead.[7]

This story is disturbing to our sense of justice, but it was not absurd to those who, in this primitive fashion, responded to that

[6] See, for example, Numbers 4:15–20; Exodus 3:1–5.
[7] II Samuel 6:1–8; cf. I Samuel 6:19 ff.

which was for them *kadosh*. The great classical scholar Gilbert Murray was particularly unhappy with this tale:

> If he [Uzzah] was struck dead by the sheer holiness of the tabu object, the holiness stored inside it like so much electricity, his death was a misfortune, an interesting accident and no more. But when it is made into the deliberate act of an anthropomorphic God, who strikes a well-intentioned man dead in explosive rage for a very pardonable mistake, a dangerous element has been introduced into the ethics of that religion. A being who is the moral equal of man must not behave like a charge of dynamite.[8]

Murray is right in his protest but wrong in his sequence. The element to which he objects was not being "introduced" at this point. It was, rather, imbedded in a primitive story reflecting an earlier view of the *kadosh*. The prophetic view of an ethical God who is himself *kadosh* was yet to be developed.

An intermediate step in this development involved the communicability of *kedushah*. Contact with that which was *kadosh* was in these instances not fatal but rendered the contacting party himself *kadosh* and, thus, separated or set aside for the service of God.[9] This layer of meaning will be seen to persist effectively in the fully developed symbolism of the value-term itself.

The miraculous, revolutionary insight that was to shape all later Judaism was that the *Kadosh* was not something found in designated objects or persons but was a property of or identical with the universal God. This radical idea seems to have burst with dramatic force upon one man: Isaiah of Jerusalem in the eighth century B.C.E. It was Isaiah who coined the phrase *"K'dosh Yisrael:* the *Kadosh* of Israel" and identified that *kadosh* of Israel with the Lord God, in contrast to the material and magical view of the *kadosh* that was held by pagan wor-

[8] Gilbert Murray, *Five Stages of Greek Religion* (London: Watts and Co., 1946), p. 68. Compare Salomon Reinach, *Orpheus* (New York: Horace Liveright, 1930), p. 4.

[9] Exodus 13:2, 29:37; Leviticus 6:11. As in Deuteronomy 23:18, this meaning of the term can frequently be found in the use of the words *k'daysha* and *kadesh* for the female and male prostitutes of Canaanite religion.

shipers.[10] He himself describes in appropriately poetic imagery the moment of revelation, when he stood in the great Temple, felt it filled with the divine presence and cried out in a transport of religious ecstasy: *"Kadosh, kadosh, kadosh* is the Lord of Hosts whose glory fills the entire world!" [11]

Isaiah went further. After associating his sense of presence, described by the word *kadosh,* with the one God, he boldly proclaimed man's responsibility for establishing that presence. "God who is *kadosh* becomes *kadosh* through the righteous action of human beings," he declared.[12]

The stage is now set for the brilliant extension of the idea in the nineteenth chapter of Leviticus and in the doctrine of *kiddush hashem* developed by the later prophets and by the rabbinic tradition.

The opening statement of Leviticus 19 has always been a stumbling block. Usually translated, "Ye shall be holy for I the Lord thy God am holy," its meaning has been sought without reference to the entire chapter that it heads. We are told that it is an address to the children of Israel telling them that they are to be *p'rushim,* separated or set aside just as God is separate and apart.[13] This violates the spirit of the normative tradition for the sake of a solution to the problems set by a difficult verse. Neither God nor man is viewed by Judaism as susceptible of isolation. The later commentators echo that interpretation without adequately dealing with its enforced view of God as "separate" as well. One contemporary scholar tells us that the word *kadosh* means the "absolute transcendence" of God.[14] But this leads to absurdities, not least of which is the task of interpreting the verse with which we are concerned: "Ye shall be absolutely transcendent . . ."! It is also an interpretation that is vitiated by the frequency with which the prophets find the *Kadosh* in the

10 Isaiah 30:15.

11 Isaiah 6:3.

12 Isaiah 5:16; cf. 8:11 ff.

13 In the discussion of this passage found in the Sifra, an expository commentary on Leviticus, ascribed to the second century.

14 Israel Efros, "Holiness and Glory in the Bible," *Jewish Quarterly Review,* XLI (April 1951), 363 ff.

midst of the people, functioning as the most immanent kind of presence.[15]

The meaning of the verse must be sought in the content of Leviticus 19. Read it first, without tranlation of the key terms, as a topical sentence: "You are *k'doshim,* as I the Lord thy God am *kadosh.*" Now scan the ethical injunctions that make up the greater part of the chapter: Leave your gleanings for the poor and the stranger; do not steal, or deal falsely, or lie to one another; do not oppress your neighbor or keep your employees' wages overnight; do not curse the deaf or put stumbling blocks in the way of the blind; be fair in judgment; do not be a tale-bearer; do not hate, or take vengeance, or bear grudges; but *love your neighbor as yourself*—especially the stranger, "For ye were strangers in the land of Egypt; I am the Lord your God." [16]

All these injunctions have to do with the relationship between man and man, and all reflect a view of relationship founded upon *respect.* Significantly, too, each injunction is followed by the reiterated reminder: "I am the Lord." The pattern is clear: because all men are *k'doshim* as God is *kadosh,* every man demands respect for the presence—the reflection of divinity, the preciousness of potentiality, the supreme value of human life—that is within him, just as the overarching and inclusive presence, the *Kadosh* that is God, demands respect. One may, therefore, read the opening statement of the chapter, "That value-presence *(kadosh)* which is found in Me is also to be found in each and everyone of you." [17] This interpretation throws new light on the protest of that indomitable rebel, Korach, whose summary execution caused the entire community to murmur against Moses. Korach gives expression to the essence of the democratic ideal when he says to Moses, "You take too much upon yourself—all of the members of the community are

---

[15] See Hosea 11:9; Ezekiel 39:7.

[16] Verses 9–18 and 32–37 seem to me to be the original core of Leviticus 19, into which ritual and prophetic regulations have been inserted.

[17] The Hebrew *"K'doshim tih'yu,"* usually translated "Ye *shall be* holy," presents no problem. The imperfect tense often expresses a state of being rather than a future connotation, as in *"Ehyeh asher ehyeh*— I am what I am" in Exodus 3:14.

k'doshim, every one of them, and God's presence is among them—you have no right to exalt yourself. . . ." [18]

This assertion that the *Kadosh,* the Presence, is to be found in human beings provides the background for Ben Azzai's choice of the first verse of the fifth chapter of Genesis as the most all-inclusive verse in Scripture: "This is the book of the generations of Man: in the day that God created man, in the likeness of God made He him." His election of this idea as most important is underscored in the same Midrash [19] by a fourth-century teacher:

> See that thou do not say, "Inasmuch as I have been despised, my fellow shall be despised with me, inasmuch as I have been cursed, my fellow shall be cursed with me." Rabbi Tanchuma said, "If thou doest this, reflect Whom thou dost despise: In the likeness of God made He him."

This is a conscious and radical reversal of the normal human psychological mechanism of projection—the impulse, when you have had a hurt, to pass it on. It is a reversal founded on the distinctive Jewish concept of *kedusha* that made possible the "slaves in Egypt" motif that runs through Jewish literature and liturgy: "You know the very being (*nefesh*) of the stranger, seeing you were strangers in the land of Egypt," *therefore* "the stranger you shall not oppress." [20]

When we recognize the Divine Presence in other human beings we are bound to respond to it and to establish *kedusha* in relationships. This is the interpretation that I customarily give to the traditional formula spoken by the groom as he puts the ring on the bride's finger in the Jewish marriage ceremony: "*Haray at m'koodeshet li* . . . Behold thou art become *kadosh* for me." The common interpretation would be that the bride is now "separated" from all others and "tabu" to other men. But this is not the meaning of *kadosh* in its fullness. I read it to mean: "In thee I find that Divine Presence that demands of me

[18] Numbers 16:3 ff.

[19] Genesis Rabba 24,7 and Theodor's note, ad loc. (Ben Azzai is a second-century sage.)

[20] Exodus 23:9.

respect and receptivity. I see thee as the bearer of that precious uniqueness and potentiality that is the 'likeness of God.' "

Kedusha, like the other distinctive cluster-words of Judaism, has a reciprocal character that establishes it as a factor of relationship. Just as *mitzvah* is both the divine address and the human response, and a *b'racha* [21] both proceeds from the divine and is bestowed upon the divine, so God is both made *kadosh* by man's action and bestows *kedusha* upon man: "I am the Lord who makes you *kadosh.*" [22] Indeed the commentators say "If you make yourselves *kadosh* I account it unto you as if you had made Me *kadosh.*" [23]

The notion that man has the capacity to affect the *kedusha* of God is a strange one. The essential nature of divinity cannot be touched by human action. The concept tells us, however, that men are responsible for the way in which the Divine Presence is recognized in the world of men. This is how the twin ideas of *kiddush hashem* and *kiddush hachaim,* the focal motivations of Jewish ethics, came into being. *Hashem* means "the name," and it may stand for the divine reputation, or, as a substitute expression for the ineffable name and as an avoidance of blatant anthropomorphism, it may stand for God Himself. Hence, *kiddush hashem* means making God present or protecting God's reputation by one's actions. For obvious reasons, it came to be, after centuries of persecution, a synonym for martyrdom—to die *al kiddush hashem* constituting the ultimate form of testimony. The opposite concept, *chillul hashem* [24] meant the destruction of the divine reputation or an act that leads to God's *absence*—in essence, it meant, and means today, a public denial in words or action of the presence of God.

The idea that the divine reputation is placed in human hands gave the Jew a double ethical motivation among the nations. To defraud anyone is a sin, and for a Jew to defraud a Jew is just that. However, were a Jew to defraud a non-Jew it would be

[21] Customarily translated "blessing." Its root is *berech* or "knee," and I find in the varied uses of the word a kind of reciprocal choreography.

[22] Leviticus 22:32–33.

[23] In the Sifra discussion of this passage.

[24] See Leviticus 22:31–32; cf. Ezekiel 20:9–12.

the sin of fraud *plus* the sin of *chillul hashem*. This is illustrated in a quaint story told of Shim'on ben Shetach, a teacher who was one of the most important Pharisees of the first century B.C.E. It is said that his disciples purchased a donkey from an Arab, and when they delivered it to him, Shim'on found a valuable jewel in its ear. His disciples, motivated by his poverty, argued that it was rightfully his and urged him to keep it. Shim'on responded, "You purchased a donkey, not a jewel," and he insisted that they return it. When the Arab received his jewel back, he cried out, "Blessed be the God of Shim'on ben Shetach!" [25]

Kiddush hachaim, the second derivative concept, means infusing *all* of life with the divine presence. Everything a human being does, including the necessary physical acts and the sensual joys of life, can be done with such respect for life and for human values that it insures the presence of God. Among the Cabalists and the Chassidim of the modern era, this means releasing the sparks of *kedusha* from the husks of materiality that imprison them.

This view of life and of man's obligation is antithetical to the mechanization of human beings in an ant-heap society, no matter how efficient it might be. Life devoid of wonder, empty of emotion, in which human beings are the expendable parts of an organized structure, even if that structure provides the satisfaction of physical wants, would be life in which the fulfillment of human possibilities would be frustrated. It would be life empty of *kedusha*, in which the unique worth of each individual—every one of them carrying the likeness of God—would not be realized; the divine image would be smothered. A third-century teacher said that man outweighs the entire world.[26] In the secular city freed of the demands made by Judaeo-Christian value, the world would outweigh man.

The connection between *kedusha*—the sense of the Divine Presence in man and the effort to infuse it into life—and the precious elements of consciousness and value that lend life sig-

[25] Tractate *Baba Metzia* of the Jerusalem Talmud, II, 8c.
[26] Rabbi Abba b. Kahana. Talmud, Tractate *Berachot* 6b (Soncino translation, p. 30).

nificance are illustrated in a picture drawn by the American poet-philosopher, George Santayana. If consciousness is accessory to life and not essential to it, Santayana says, we could posit a mechanical world in which there would be perfect organization of the useful reactions of automata without a single sensation. It would be a dumb show invested with the appearance of the pursuit of conceived goods. In such a mechanized world, however, there would be no element of value; in removing consciousness we have removed the possibility of worth.

Santayana goes further. He offers us a "less violent abstraction":

> . . . a world of beings of purely intellectual cast, minds in which the transformations of nature were mirrored without any emotion. Every event would then be noted, its relations would be observed; its recurrence might even be expected; but all this would happen without a shadow of desire, of pleasure or regret. No event would be repulsive, no situation terrible—all values and excellence gone just as much as if consciousness were absent. For the existence of good we need not merely consciousness but emotional consciousness.

What he meant by "emotional consciousness" may be more deeply apprehended in the soft focus of his well-known lines, "It is not wisdom to be only wise." Santayana's "poetic naturalism" made room for a reverent appreciation of that which lies beyond the grasp of sense and intellect—it joined nature with "supernature" in a dynamic continuity, in which value and the wisdom of the "heart" may exist.

Combine this "emotional consciousness" of Santayana with Albert Schweitzer's "reverence for life" and crown them with a recognition of the supreme worth of the human individual, and the task of *kiddush hachaim*—infusing life with the presence—is defined. It is a task for the ordinary man, in his everyday life: to open himself to the *Kadosh* and to seek in every moment to respond to its demands.

Were that sense of presence to abide completely among men, the "latter days" of peace and security envisioned by Isaiah and

Micah would be at hand. Violence and war are a denial of that presence, even a destruction of it. Poverty and degradation, states in which men cannot abide "each under his own vine and his own fig-tree with none to make him afraid," are affronts to *kedusha*. Race hatred, prejudice, and denial of opportunity to those of different skin color or background is contemning the likeness of God.

The major doxology of Jewish liturgy, the *kaddish*—closely paralleled by the Lord's Prayer of Christianity—begins with an invocation of *Kiddush hashem,* asking that God's great name be made *kadosh* and that His presence be manifested in the speedy establishment of His Kingdom upon earth. This is not an accidental connection. When we perceive the *kadosh* in every other human being, we are led to seek a society in which *kedushah* will mark all relationships. True community arises out of respect for persons. But to exalt the organization of society over the individuals who comprise it is to block ourselves off from the Presence, from that which is of highest human value. John Macmurray presents this insight to us in somewhat different form, when he writes:

> To feel for the state, or for the Nation, the kind of reverence . . . that is appropriate to persons, is an emotional unreason, the very essence of superstition. To worship the State is to indulge in idolatry. To personify the State is to pervert it so that it tends to the destruction of society . . . To create community . . . is a religious task which can only be performed through the transformation of the motives of our behavior.[27]

Worship of the State is worship of the structure—the most pervasive idolatry of our time. It is a worship impossible to those who make *kiddush hashem* and *kiddush hachaim* the central motivations of their lives, for the effort to establish the divine presence leads harmoniously into the metaphors of the Kingship and the Kingdom of God.

[27] John Macmurray, *Persons In Relation* (New York: Harper & Row, 1961), p. 198.

Admittedly, these are metaphors that seem to be out of consonance with the spirit of our age. We have dethroned all kings, and we chafe at the continued existence even of titular thrones. We are a democracy or a republic, and we tolerate with some amusement the existence of a Queen of England and "kingship" in those countries that espouse royalty as a form. Actually, the imagery, as Biblical religion uses it, is quite the reverse of "undemocratic." It says to us that our loyalty can be commanded by no *human* king, by *no* state, by *no* earthly power, but that we admit of only one authority, and that is the ultimate authority of God.

Somewhere, Sholem Asch tells the story of a Jewish galley slave in the time of the Roman Empire who amazed his captors, for he served in the galley an incredibly long period of time, while those about him who were chained to the same benches died or went mad. Nothing could break his spirit. And he kept muttering through his great beard, "*L'cha adonai hamamlacha*— Thine alone, O Lord, is the kingdom." The overseer of the captives would say, "Stubborn Jews, let them get an idea between their teeth and they will worry it and worry it and nothing can shake it from them." But the slave continued in unbroken faithfulness, saying through his suffering, "*L'cha adonai hamamlacha!*"

The kingship of God, the *malchut shaddai* (or the *malchut shamaim,* which is the same concept) is not something in the distant future. It exists, if only men would acknowledge it. "*Yikablu alayem et ol malchutecha . . .*" If they would take upon themselves the yoke of God's kingship, a messianic age of peace and of justice would be ushered in. What this metaphor does is to find authority only in those ultimate demands of justice and love and of truth that we associate with God.

A *melech* was a tribal chieftain. If the tribes were united into a nation and later into an empire, he became a *melech m'lachim*— a king of kings—a national king or an emperor such as the emperor of the Babylonians or the Persians. But the Jew bowed down only before the *melech mal'chay ham'lachim*—the one who is the *King of the Kings of Kings:* a hyperbole, in imagery that was familiar, for Him whose authority stands above *all* earthly authority. It is an imagery that must lead to the insight that every created being stands in the same relationship to this divine sovereignty as does every other created being.

In the prayer that gives expression to this concept, we proclaim the ultimate triumph of justice, of brotherhood, and of love, when all men will acknowledge God's kingship *"v'haya adonai l'melech al kol ha'aretz*—and God will be King over all the earth." When we use this metaphor and proclaim God as King, we give expression to our willingness to yield *only* to the highest authority. Thus our *yielding* means our *resistance!* It means resistance to all that is contingent, to all idolatries, to all tyranny, to all error, to all evil.

"God's kingship" is, of course, a liturgical and traditional metaphor. It grew out of a conscious search to find words that would associate ultimate authority with felt presence. Its structured form does not, however, depreciate its value. Its poetry, like the poetry of *kedusha* out of which it flows, both gives us the means to express what we have experienced and reciprocally reinforces and enriches the value-content of that experience. From the sense of presence, which has been universally present in human experience, we come to an obligation to respond to the abiding and most significant presence, as it is manifested in our fellow human beings. And from experiencing it in our fellows, we come to be able to open ourselves to the presence of the divine.

The German word for "presence" is *"Gegenwart"* or "that which waits over against us." This evokes for me the other side of the coin. If we can but be fully present in the present moment to all that presents itself to us, then we may hear its address: the address of our fellows, the address of our world, the address of God. In the relationships that are immediate we may find a reflection of that relationship that is ultimate. We want to explore the nature of that possibility now.

CHAPTER TEN

RELATIONSHIP IS THE KEY

Kedusha is found in relationship, the twofold relationship that marks the religious life: *bayn adam l'chavayro,* between man and his fellow; *bayn adam lamakom,* between man and divinity. It is uncovered by dynamic action: the act of turning toward one's fellow or turning toward God; the act of righteousness that releases the inherent *kedusha* in the world, which in effect reveals the presence of the divine.

The beginning of the religious life is in the "hallowing" of relationships. Indeed, the experience of relationship is the beginning of all thought and the essential element in the establishment of personality, the discovery of the ego.

"In the beginning is relation." [1]

John Hersey, in *The Child Buyer,* a not-so-fantastic *"mene-tekel"* utopian work of fiction, describes the calculated conversion of a child into a computing machine. The first step in the process is the withdrawal of the child from all experience of relationship. He is "placed naked in a bare and confined chamber, six feet cubed, without exterior lighting, dimly lit within, so that the consciousness can take in nothing but the totality of barrenness of the setting. There is nothing. There is silence." [2] With nothing to respond to, the child is emptied of all knowledge, of all acquired habits and skills.

Hersey's fantasy is the womb—the prenatal environment in

[1] Martin Buber, *I and Thou*, 2nd ed. (New York: Charles Scribner's Sons, 1958), p. 18.

[2] John Hersey, *The Child Buyer* (New York: Alfred A. Knopf, 1960), p. 204.

143

which the Self in any meaningful sense is not existent. The Self
is formed by its responses to that which is other than Self. This
is the existential fact that lies behind Martin Buber's affirmation
that "All real living is meeting."

Buber's presentation of a philosophy of relation is not structured in the conventional systematic manner—and intentionally
so. The heart of what he wishes to teach is revealed only when
we avoid the traps of steno-language and approach him with
that openness and receptivity that are themselves the distinguishing marks of the Buberian stance.

There is, however, an interesting parallel to Martin Buber,
presented in the more conventional philosophical style of John
Macmurray, the lucid and persuasive Scottish teacher who, in
his Gifford Lectures,[3] systematically sets forth the nature of
relationship and its theological implications. Both Buber, who
has denied the label, and Macmurray, to whom it has probably
never been applied, are "existentialist" thinkers in that their
starting point is the experience of the individual human being.
This is the Cartesian heritage of modern man—that he no longer
attempts to impose a structure on the cosmos into which he
then seeks to fit his experience, but rather that he begins with
his experience. Someone, recently, has spoken of "theology
working its way upward." It would seem more correct to call
it theology working its way *outward*—from the individual to
the cosmos. Even that description needs a further limitation in
a definition of man's experience, which includes his relationship
to his group experience—the traditions and the environmental
influences that shape his value-stance—and his experience of
the cosmos.

Both Buber and Macmurray make explicit this role of community and thus break through the terrible isolation into which
the existentialism of Kierkegaard and Sartre would plunge man.
The individual is not totally alone and unaided. Buber's great

[3] John Macmurray, *The Self as Agent* (London: Faber and Faber,
1957) and *Persons In Relation* (New York: Harper & Row, 1961). These
represent Volumes I and II of *The Form of the Personal*.

answer to Kierkegaard, "The Question to the Single One," [4] makes this clear. For although Buber affirms that the individual must ultimately make his decisions and must distinguish in his "innermost being" between what is commanded him and what is not commanded him, he also makes room for the total inherited experience of the group of which the individual is part and for the effect upon him of the needs of that group and the direction of that group. There is no way, short of a flight into authoritarianism, to free modern man of his ultimate responsibility to decide. The decision may, however, be made in the midst of community and not without regard for the interests of the community. Buber writes:

> I experience what God desires of me for this hour—so far as I do experience it—not earlier than *in* the hour . . . With my choice and decision and action—committing or omitting, acting or persevering—I answer the word, however inadequately, yet properly; I answer for my hour. My group cannot relieve me of this responsibility . . . I do not in the least mean that a man must fetch the answer alone and unadvised out of his breast . . . He must find his way to that responsibility armed with all the "ought" that has been forged in the group. . . .[5]

Here, as in all the paradoxes of life, man must walk the "narrow ridge" between his aloneness and his existence in community. His relationship to his fellow men will be the path along which he comes to confront the Ultimate Demand—"The extended lines of relations meet in the eternal *Thou*. Every particular *Thou* is a glimpse through to the eternal Thou" [6]—but when he stands before that demand he stands armed with the inherited "ought"—and alone with the other pole of ultimate relationship.

Relationship is the central fact of the definition of Self, whether it deals with that which is immediately present or that which is ultimately present. Here is where we encounter the

[4] Martin Buber, *Between Man and Man* (New York: The Macmillan Company, 1965), pp. 40–82.

[5] *Between Man and Man*, pp. 68 f.

[6] *I and Thou*, p. 75.

contemporary inadequacy of the great philosophic systems, especially those of Descartes and of Kant. "Any philosophy which takes the "Cogito" [7] as its starting point and centre of reference institutes a formal dualism of theory and practice;" says Macmurray, "And . . . this dualism makes it formally impossible to give any account, and indeed to conceive the possibility of persons in relation, whether the relation be theoretical—as knowledge, or practical—as cooperation. For thought is essentially private." [8]

Macmurray, taking action as the opposite of thought, shatters this dualism by substituting *"Ago"* for *"Cogito"*: I *act,* therefore I am; rather than, I *think,* therefore I am. That we would more adequately apprehend the importance of relationship by broadening Macmurray's proposal and saying *"Respondeo"*—I *respond,* therefore I am—should become apparent as this exposition develops.

Like Buber, Macmurray speaks of the relationship between the Self and the Other, rather than between subject and object. This is more than a verbal matter. It is a necessary distinction when the standpoint of relationship replaces the standpoint of thought:

> The Self as agent is an existent, and its correlative therefore, is also in existence . . . In a particular case the Other may be another thing or another organism or another person.[9]

When I act and encounter the "resistance" of the Other, then I define the Self—become conscious that I am I.

In Buber, too, the Self is defined by the Other, but the phrase "resistance to action" would not adequately describe what takes place; rather, it is "awareness" that characterizes the Self, and the relationship takes place in the "between-ness" that is neither the Self nor the Other. This is so because Buber makes a fruitful distinction between two primary forms of response. The first

[7] Meaning "I think." This would include the various forms of positivism.
[8] *The Self as Agent,* p. 73.
[9] *The Self as Agent,* p. 106.

is characterized by the combination "I-Thou," the second by "I-It."

"I-It" is the common state of man essential to life and growth, getting and begetting, using and spending. It is the relationship of operation, whether that operation is the infant's drawing of nourishment from the mother or the scholar's communication of an idea. "I-Thou" is the relationship of total awareness, when the "I" is totally present to the Other, whether the Other is thing or organism, intellectual form or aesthetic form. It is this latter, for Buber, that most fully deserves the adjective "personal."

The child in the womb knows no relationship. It rests in an "undivided primal world." From the moment of birth, the child seeks relationship, "hands sketch delicately and dimly in the empty air." This is "the correspondence of the child . . . with what is alive and effective over against it." This occurs even when it is not action for an end—simply the instinct to respond to the "inborn Thou," the a priori of relation. Through the "Thou," both the mutual relation that is tenderness and the personification that makes address and response possible, develop. Through the "Thou," the "I" becomes an "I." [10]

True relationship inheres in "I-Thou," for in "I-It" there is an element of separation, of distance. Therefore, for Buber, all "I-Thou" relationship is mutual. Macmurray makes *all* relationship reciprocal:

> The possibility of action depends upon the Other being also agent, and so upon a plurality of agents in one field of action. The resistance to the Self through which the Self can exist as agent must be the resistance of another self . . . the "I do"—the fact that there is action—is the primary centainty.[11]

[10] *I and Thou*, pp. 25–28. Compare this with Chapter Two of *Persons In Relation*, especially pp. 56–57. How this process may eventually result in realizing the Other as person, the prerequisite of dialogue, is more formally set forth by Buber in his essay "Distance and Relation," reprinted in *The Knowledge of Man*, ed. Maurice S. Friedman (New York: Harper & Row, 1965), pp. 59 ff.

[11] *The Self as Agent*, p. 145.

From this position, Macmurray's argument moves carefully and formally to the assertion that it is possible to "think the world as one action" and "to think a Supreme Agent whose act the world is." [12]

This, however, is what Buber would call talking *about* God rather than *to* God. God is not inferred from Buber's exposition of relationship. He is properly "only addressed, not expressed" [13]—the relationship must itself be experienced, not argued into existence. This is the frustration that makes Buber's style of writing essential to him. We, on the other hand, bound on the wheel of discursive thought, are reduced in this exposition to talking "about God" and to demonstrating how it is possible to do so.

The crucial point of difference between Buber and Macmurray lies here. It is also the point at which Macmurray is bound to fail in the effort to find anchorage for the structure of humanitarian and democratic values that he obviously prefers. That which is central in Buber, even to the point of giving form to relationship and to actions, is the *word*. Relationship is dialogue. The Self is addressed and responds. The relationship to the eternal Thou is also one of address and response. This "Thou which can never become an It" is not a formally projected supreme agent in whose action we participate, but the "Thou" that is the source of *mitzvah*, of command. It is a "Thou" whose address man experiences, a "Thou" who makes demands upon man.

Macmurray's personalism eventuates in no greater ethical absolute than the "harmonious interrelation of agents" that is the community. The rigor of a divine demand is replaced by a Kantian imperative: "Act always as a legislating member of a Kingdom of Ends." [14] Thus morality becomes the problematic of personal relations, and the effort to ground our values in that very *kedusha* that marks Macmurray's idea of interpersonal relationships is not helped by his characterization of that prob-

[12] *The Self as Agent*, pp. 220–222.
[13] *I and Thou*, pp. 80 f.
[14] *Persons In Relation*, p. 119.

lematic as "religious." Says Macmurray, "My care for you is only moral if it includes the intention to preserve your freedom as an agent which is your independence of me." [15]

But this is no more solid than what is given us by nontheistic philosophers of value or than the aphorism of Oliver Wendell Holmes, Jr., that "my freedom to swing my arms ends where your nose begins." Ralph Barton Perry, too, speaks of "harmonious happiness," [16] the kind of consensus that is present in a Quaker meeting. But that consensus is achieved only when there is an antecedent and accepted structure of values that makes harmony itself a good and that makes the happiness of the Other essential to that harmony. Hence, "the harmonious interrelation of agents" begs the central question with which a philosophy of value must be concerned.

When we stand in relationship with a universal God whose presence or whose potential presence we experience in our fellow human beings and in the world, we stand in relationship with that increasing harmony, growing coherence, and developing refinement of consciousness that is written—as we have asserted earlier—into the very constitution of the universe, as it is characterized by the direction of cosmic evolution. The demand of that God in the high religions—often misinterpreted and bitterly misused by imperfect man—has always and not surprisingly been a demand for love, justice, and respect for the worth of the human person. The experience of that address by a historic group of committed people must eventuate, as it often has, in a value-stance that includes compassion, equity, and a recognition of the supreme value of life—life waiting to be infused with the divine presence.

Why then have we seen so much more frequently in human history a lack of compassion, an absence of equity, and the cruel destruction of life? This question is the one most used as

---

[15] *Persons In Relation*, p. 190.

[16] Ralph Barton Perry, *Realms of Value* (Cambridge, Mass: Harvard University Press, 1954), pp. 132 ff. Perry, himself, recognizes the inherent potential confusion of interests, e.g., "What is good for General Motors is good for the United States."

a weapon against God-talk and God-relationship. It must be
answered with a clear recognition of the fact that not all who
cry "The Temple of the Lord, the Temple of the Lord" are
turning toward the Presence. It is *men* who fail to perceive the
kadosh in their fellows or who fail to hear its address in the
world. The failure to turn is a failure of sensitivity. It is the
Neo-Neanderthal type who glorifies his own image or sinks
himself in things who blocks himself off from genuine relationship.

Martin Buber quite properly speaks of turning as the physical,
almost the muscular act [17]—really as a technique to achieve
the prerequisite disposition of Self, the "releasing" of the inhibiting bands that permits us to open ourselves to the Presence.
"The life of dialogue is no privilege of intellectual activity . . .
it begins no higher than where humanity begins. There are no
gifted and ungifted here, only those who give themselves and
those who withhold themselves." [18]

The "I-It" category makes no demand upon the emotions.
When I use a person or an object as a thing, I depersonalize
him or it; I am indifferent to that which is person. The man who
"straightforwardly hates" is closer to relationship than the "man
without hate and love." [19] Macmurray's equivalent of "I-It" is
impersonal relationship, one of two different "emotional attitudes to the other, which provide the motives for two different
ways of behaving in relation to the Other, and therefore, in the
reflective aspect of action, in conceiving the Other . . . If one
person treats another person impersonally, he treats him as if
he were an object and not a person." [20]

Although both approaches seem to tend toward the same end,
the present-ness of the Self to the Other in its uniqueness as
person, there are distinct advantages in the Buberian approach.
First, Buber's primary-word categories also include the possibility of our responding in personal terms to that which is

[17] *Between Man and Man,* p. 22.
[18] *Between Man and Man,* p. 35.
[19] *I and Thou,* p. 16.
[20] *Persons In Relation,* p. 33.

thought of as impersonal: the art object, the tree, the symphony, the pen that signed the Civil Rights Act. I can be wholly present to them and, in effect, say "Thou" to them. Because I am being wholly present to the presence in each of them, I can learn to be wholly present to the Ultimate Presence; because I can say "Thou" to each of them, I can say "Thou" to the Eternal Thou. Macmurray's stress on the interrelationship between and among agents, each having its own intention, restricts that which may be called "personal" and eventuates only in the "possibility" of "thinking" our relation to the world as a personal relation and "through the form of the personal" thinking of it as the act of a Supreme Agent.

Making action rather than response the defining factor in relationship has another limitation. It makes action the determinative of right and wrong and neglects that significant category of evil that is found in *inaction*.[21] The sins of omission—*not* doing, *not* helping, *not* responding, *not* caring—are possibly the most egregious sins. For Buber, too, the deed is decisive, but it must be a response of the total being. The "inmost essence of evil" is "decisionlessness," the failure of a human being to direct and make the most of his distinctive potentialities [22]—the failure to respond with the *kedusha* within him to the *kedusha* of the Other.

The dynamic of dialogue is such that although it can be complete without speech, it cannot be complete without action. For that to which we respond inevitably makes its demand upon us, and that demand, even if it is minimal as in the demand for attention, can be met only by an act, even so slight an act as "turning toward." Dialogue both flows from action and eventuates in action. The word is fulfilled in the deed.

This is the significance of the response of the people of Israel as they stood in the primary Encounter at Mount Sinai. They did not say "We will listen first and then we will act." This is what, according to an old legend, all the other peoples of man-

---

[21] See *Persons in Relation,* pp. 112 f.
[22] Maurice S. Friedman, *Martin Buber: The Life of Dialogue* (Chicago: University of Chicago Press, 1955), pp. 32 f., 106.

kind did. They listened first, and then, finding fault with specific aspects of the divine address that did not comport with their ways of life, they rejected the Covenant. But the response of the people of Israel was immediate: "We will *do* and we will listen." [23] The act of turning, of dedication, came first. The details could be spelled out later. When the whole being is totally present, the spoken word in its literal sense is not essential to the dialogue. What is essential, is *relationship*.

The favorite maxim inscribed over the Ark of Covenant in synagogues has long been "Know Before Whom Thou Standest." What is over-against-us as we stand in worship may be variously described. It is the Torah, the parchment scrolls of the Pentateuch in which the divine demand is set forth. But it is more. The personal pronoun indicates that the referent is the Source of that divine demand. The worshiper must know Whom he confronts. What is essential, is relationship.

It is true for Buber, as it was for Halevi, that we find God only by the act of going out to meet Him, only by the act of opening ourselves to His presence.[24] Entering into this relation is entering into absolute relation that does not exclude the world—"Everything is gathered up in the relation." When we separate God and the world we are using the language of *It*. God is "wholly Other," but he is also "wholly Present." "If you explore the life of things and of conditioned beings you come to the unfathomable," Buber writes. "If you deny the life of things and of conditioned being you stand before nothingness, if you hallow this life you meet the living God." [25]

What Buber here expresses in deliberately soft-focus terms, Macmurray says directly and, in this instance, to the same effect.

> The scientist—and, of course, the ordinary man when he is using things to achieve his purposes—limits his attention to the impersonal aspect of the world, and so excludes its personal aspect. On the other hand, if we apperceive the world personally, its impersonal aspect is not excluded. It is necessary to the constitution of

23 Exodus 24:7.
24 *I and Thou*, p. 76.
25 *I and Thou*, p. 79.

its personal character. The religious apperception is inclusive and adequate; the scientific exclusive and inadequate.[26]

The relationship with God is neither a "feeling of dependence," nor is it mystic absorption. "Feelings" are relative psychological matters, but the relation of which we speak is absolute relation. Mystic absorption is an escape from life, but this relationship is life-affirming: ". . . we with holy care wish to foster the holy good of our reality, that is gifted to us for this and perhaps for no other life that is nearer truth." [27] Nor is it a relationship easily spoken of and glibly defined, or a relationship to be used as a "gimmick" by someone who knows God as something by which he is to profit. "Woe to the man so possessed that he thinks he possesses God!" [28]

We must search out the meaning of our ultimate relationship in our relationship with other people. There we find the possibility of address and response that gives us an accessible "simile" for our relationship to the divine. It is more than a simile; it is a gate; the main portal.[29] Here is the heart of the messianic hope: in perfecting our relationship with men, we find our way to the perfection of absolute relationship; in building the perfected community, we have an echo of absolute harmony—for we are bringing the Divine Presence into the life of the world.

This is the very antithesis of the agonized resignation found frequently in atheistic existentialism. "Hell," says Sartre, "is other people." [30] But a personalist such as Buber or Macmurray says that if we could but perfect our relationship to other people, the longed-for redemption will have been achieved. "Religion would then be simply the celebration of communion—of the fellowship of all things in God. Meanwhile, it sustains the intention to achieve this fellowship." [31]

These are the alternatives that Macmurray sets before us.

---

26 *Persons In Relation*, p. 220.
27 *I and Thou*, pp. 81, 89.
28 *I and Thou*, pp. 106–107.
29 *I and Thou*, p. 103.
30 In his play, *No Exit*.
31 *Persons In Relation*, p. 165.

He tells us that where "atheistic existentialism finds human relationship an insoluble problem and all human projects doomed
to frustration and ultimate meaninglessness," we can find meaning in the "theistic alternative which issues in the hope of an
ultimate unity of persons in fellowship. . . ." [32]

Too little and too tentative! The cognitive approach of speculative philosophy—"talking *about* God"—gives us only a "hope"
of ultimate unity. The divine address experienced in Buber's
"lived relationship" *demands* of us persistence in the effort to
build that unity: when "God will be King over all the earth . . .
one and His name one." That future is not certain, it must be
said. The covenant relationship assigns a role to man who is
"m'shutaf l'ha-Kadosh baruch hu," a co-worker with the Eternal
Kadosh, blessed be He.[33]

Life and death, blessing and curse, are the true alternatives
dependent on man's decision, even though the divine demand is
"Choose life!" This was the stark black-and-white of Biblical
faith. It is infinitely more poignant today, in an age characterized by Günther Anders as the "last age," when man has placed
in his hands the power of ultimate destruction. No matter how
long it is prolonged, because man can never unlearn the thermonuclear secret, it will always be the last age. Man will have the
final say—man open to the Presence, or man blocking it off.

This is the eternal struggle between two kinds of demand—
the demand of things against the demand of that which is ultimately significant; the expedient, the pragmatic here and now,
versus the enduring purpose. "How powerful is the unbroken
world of *It,* and how delicate are the appearances of the *Thou.*" [34]
We do not open ourselves to the Presence simply by verbalizing
a will to do so. "As far as the East is from the West, so far has
He removed [the cessation of] our transgressions from us!" [35] It
is true that the distance from East to West is, so far as the individual is concerned, no more than *"ein drey"*—just a simple

[32] *The Self as Agent,* p. 222.
[33] See Friedman, *Martin Buber: The Life of Dialogue,* p. 252.
[34] *I and Thou,* p. 98.
[35] A homiletical reading of Psalm 103:12.

half-turn, the act of *teshuvah:* turning. But the world and its complexities interpose themselves continually, and we fail again and again.

"He who knows God knows also very well remoteness from God, and the anguish of barrenness in the tormented heart; but he does not know the absence of God," says Buber, "it is we only who are not always there." [36]

Indeed, it is essential to the survival of man as man that we *be* there—that we respond to God's address with decisive action. Placed in our hands is the two-way key of relationship: Our relationship with our fellow men opening the portal to the presence of God; our relationship to God opening us to fruitful relationships with our fellow men. These are the two major imperatives of Biblical religion: "Love the Lord your God with all your heart, soul, and might" and "Love your neighbor as yourself." [37]

We can affirm that God lives only when God makes demands upon us. Religion will live only when it ceases to offer assurances and renews the rigor of its demands. We want now to explore the nature of that kind of religion.

[36] *I and Thou,* p. 99.
[37] See Deuteronomy 6:5, Leviticus 19:18; see also Matthew 22:37–40, Mark 12:30–31.

CHAPTER ELEVEN

A RELIGION OF DEMAND

An eminent American teacher of philosophy was making a train trip through the New England countryside many years ago and had an insight that in a quaint way illuminates our concern. It was a warm afternoon and, as he watched the landscape flashing by the window of his day coach, he was soon lulled into a state of drowsiness. Now, in those days, the railroad right-of-way in that part of the country was dotted with billboards of varying size advertising a well-known fishery. Most of them carried the simple legend in large white letters against a black background, "Gorton's Cod. No Bones At All." And as the scholar—Professor Charles A. Bennett [1]—looked up, and one of the signs appeared and disappeared, he read it in his semisomnolent state as "Gorton's God . . . No Bones At All."

Astonished for a moment, he was jolted out of his reverie by a thought profound enough to make up for the irreverence of his misreading. "That's it!" he exclaimed. "That's exactly it—no bones at all! We talk so much about the love and the care of God that we forget the God who holds the plumb line of eternal justice in his hand!"

The God of sentimental religion wraps everything in a haze of goodness and masks evil with the lyrical trust of Pippa as she passes,[2] "God's in His heaven—/All's right with the world." This is a God who has "no bones at all."

The God who has been interred by the radical theologians is

[1] The story is told by Rufus Jones in his introduction to Bennett's *A Philosophical Study of Mysticism* (New Haven: Yale University Press, 1931), p. xii.

[2] In Browning's poetic drama, the juxtaposition is intentionally ironic.

156

the God "whose eye is on the sparrow," whose providential loving care extends to every creature. But for hosts of God-affirming men through the ages, that conception of God has never lived. True, Jeremiah, and the Deuteronomist, and liturgists of all time since have proclaimed God's everlasting love;[3] they have been challenged by the writer of Job, by many of the rabbinic sages, by Maimonides, and by hosts of others.

God is the *source* of his predicament, Job steadfastly maintains. God hounds him without even giving him time to swallow his own spit. He is responsible for evil and injustice: "If it be not He, who then is it?" Job insists on speaking out of the reality of experience. He will not afford his comforters or anyone else the privilege of telling lies on God's behalf.[4] Experience says that any insistence that God's loving eye is on the sparrow is false.

In the Mishnah,[5] we read a cryptic injunction that if one who is praying says "Thy mercies extend to a bird's nest," he is to be silenced. The rabbis who discuss this in the Talmud [6] are no longer certain of its meaning but incline to the view that the attributes of God are not to be characterized as "mercies," but as *"gezerot"*—that which has been decreed or is part of the order of things. But this injunction is coupled with an equivalent prohibition against saying either "Let Thy name be remembered for the good Thou hast done" or "We give thanks, we give thanks." Despite the varying rabbinic explanations, it seems clear that the earlier sages were concerned that men should not

---

[3] Jeremiah 31:3; Deuteronomy 4:37, 7:8. The reiterated "lovingkindness" in the Psalms is of a different order. The Hebrew word is *chesed,* a difficult term more akin to grace and mercy than to love—freely given and experienced in wonder, or earned through action.

[4] Job 3:23, 6:9, 7:19, 9:22–24, 13:7. See Maimonides, *The Guide For the Perplexed,* Book III, Chapter 23; in the translation of Shlomo Pines (Chicago: University of Chicago Press, 1963), p. 490. Compare Book I, Chapter 54 (Pines translation, p. 126).

[5] The compilation of rabbinic discussions made at the close of the second century, which is the core of the Talmud. The reference here is to the section known as *Berachot* ("Blessings") V:3 (see *The Mishnah,* trans. Herbert Danby [New York: Oxford University Press, 1933], p. 6).

[6] Tractate *Berachot* 33b (Soncino translation, p. 209).

oversentimentalize their relationship to the Deity, forgetting that evil exists and overlooking the rigor that is also part of ultimate reality.

We have already discussed [7] the popular misconception of what "Law" means in Biblical religion. What we are saying here seems once again to raise the old controversy of "Law" versus "Gospel" and to contrast the sternness of Judaism with the gentleness of Christianity, the "Law" of the Old Testament with the "Love" of the New. This is a distinction rejected by competent scholars.

Normative Judaism is too deeply immersed in emotions of compassion and tenderness for anyone to be able to maintain that its lineaments are harshness or cold-bloodedness. Yet, in the Jewish reaction against Christian misinterpretation,[8] we have been too ready to identify the God of Judaism as the "God of Love," and we have therefore overlooked a crucial difference in emphasis. The God of Christianity is the God who *gives;* the God of Judaism is the God who *demands.*

The central stress of Christianity has been on the doctrine of John: "God so loved the world that he gave his only Son, that whoever believes in him should not perish but have eternal life . . . not to condemn the world but that the world might be saved through him." [9] The central stress of Judaism has been: "Thou *shalt* be unto me a Kingdom of priests," "*Choose* life!" and "Thus saith the Lord. . . ." The covenant obligation that is central in Judaism calls upon the Jew to be God's co-worker in perfecting the world—not to *be* saved but to *participate* in the redemption of mankind.

Our era derives from normative Christianity and from the dicta of contemporary reductive psychology an emphasis upon belief and upon its subjective character. The special genius of Judaism has been the fact that it is grounded not upon belief

[7] See Chapter Three (p. 37–38).

[8] See "The Law and Recent Criticism," in Solomon Schecter, *Studies in Judaism* (Philadelphia: Jewish Publication Society, 1896), pp. 233 ff. See also Schecter's *Some Aspects of Rabbinic Theology* (New York: The Macmillan Company, 1909), Chapter VIII, especially pp. 116 ff.

[9] John 3:16–17.

but upon the experience of relationship. We are not called upon
to affirm either God or God-related events, but we are called
upon to respond to God's address and to carry out His demands.[10] This is the essential difference between *b'rit,* which
is central in Judaism, and *kerygma,* which is central in Christianity. *B'rit* means covenant—a contractual *relationship* that
makes demands on those who adhere to it. *Kerygma* is an event
in time and space that must be affirmed: the apostolic pronouncement, beside the empty tomb, of the Lordship of Jesus.

This may seem to some to be a quibble. They would ask how
we can relate to God and act on His demands unless we also
"believe" in Him. Actually it is not necessary to develop a cognitive theory nor to build an intellectually refined concept in
order to experience and to respond. Belief is intellectual assent;
action is a response to the experienced address.

There is a reference in the Talmud, the significance of which
is not reduced by its laconic character, to the fact that the School
of Hillel and the School of Shammai [11] debated for two and a
half years the question of whether it would have been better if
man had never been created. It is interesting to note that not
one word of what must have been a fascinating speculative discussion is recorded in the Talmud—except for its pragmatic
conclusion. They finally wound up the discussion and took a
vote, and the decision was: perhaps it would have been better
if man had never been created, but he *has* been created—so let
him examine his *actions!* [12]

This functional emphasis of Judaism is a stance understood
by Harvey Cox insofar as Biblical faith is concerned. "Asked
about Yahweh," he says, "the average Old Testament Israelite
would never have answered in terms of metaphysical categories—

[10] See above, Chapter Two (pp. 13–14).

[11] Hillel and Shammai were two teachers who flourished at the beginning of the first century. In general, Hillel is the "optimist" and
Shammai is the "realist."

[12] Tractate *'Erubin* 13b (Soncino, p. 87). Two alternate forms of
"examine" are suggested: *y'fashpesh* and *y'mashmesh.* But the difference
between them is inconsequential. The clear meaning is that man's task
is to *act* in accord with the divine demand.

omniscience, omnipresence, and the like. He would have told
his interrogator what Yahweh had *done:* brought him up out of
the land of Egypt. . . ." [13] But this functional approach in Biblical
faith is two-sided. Under the Covenant, this ancient Israelite
was to have been aware not only of what *God* had done as
Creator and Redeemer and Lawgiver, but even more important,
he was called to an awareness of what God required *him* to do.
Cox seems to be unaware that this characteristic is found not
only in Biblical faith, but that it has marked the normative Jewish response from Egypt to the present day. A Jew is not obliged
to define, he is obliged to act. He is obliged to seek a relationship with God. He is obliged to answer the divine demand with
appropriate conduct. In that stance, men are called upon not to
"believe in the Lord," but to "know God," "to trust in God,"
to "seek God."

The word most frequently translated as "belief" in the Hebrew Bible is a verb from the root *"amen"*—the same "amen"
that is used to confirm a prayer or sentiment. The central meaning of that root is "to be firm," and so the Hebrew word *"emunah,"* usually translated by "faith," means firmness, persistence,
or unshaken trust—all of which are factors of relationship. The
Hebrew word *"yada,"* translated as "know," also implies relationship.[14] It is a relationship manifested in action, as Jeremiah's direct challenge affirms: "He judged the cause of the
poor and needy. . . . Is not this to know Me? saith the Lord." [15]
The earth will be filled with the "knowledge of the Lord" when
violence and destruction have been rooted out of it, when men
carry God's demand in their hearts.[16]

A God who is only a concept or an object of belief makes no
demands and is not existent for man in any meaningful sense.
Without demands, without address and response, we may as well

[13] Harvey Cox, *The Secular City* (New York: The Macmillan Company, 1965), p. 66, and see also p. 77.

[14] See Genesis 4:1. See also Martin Buber's study of Hebrew *"emunah"*
and Greek *"pistis"* in his *Two Types of Faith* (New York: The Macmillan Company, 1951), especially pp. 170 ff. and pp. 28–29.

[15] Jeremiah 22:16.

[16] Isaiah 11:9; Jeremiah 31:33–34.

says that God is dead. If God makes no demands, He is not God; if there is no God there are no ultimate demands.

The Deist conception that God set the world going and then abandoned it to its own resources does not speak to that aspect of human experience that relates God to the ethical quest and makes the ethical quest a universal component of religious expression. It does not comport with the experience of massive evil, either. Early Enlightenment thinkers had to conclude that God had set the world going *well* and that, therefore, morality is written into the nature of things. This led logically to Leibnitz and the "best of all possible worlds" idea with which Voltaire had such sport in *Candide*.

Only in the dynamics of address and response is it possible to confront a world filled with moral imperfections, with bestiality and brutality and horror, and to persist in the task to which we know ourselves called. God must "want" something of us and of the world.

This linkage between God's demands and the proclamation of God's death has always been present in atheism in two contrasting forms of expression: The first says that if God wants nothing, God is useless, and men are free to do what they wish. The second says that if God does want something, He has been singularly unsuccessful and, indeed, must be charged with responsibility for the pain and evil that exist in the world.[17] Thus for many death-of-God thinkers from Nietzsche to Altizer, disposing of God means disposing of moral imperatives and of the source of value-judgment. For such, as for Ivan Karamazov, everything is permitted.

We can read the first part of this argument in both directions. "Murdering God . . . ," says Richard Rubenstein, "is an assertion of the will to total moral and religious license" in any system in which all values derive from God.[18] It is also true that the death of God becomes a fact when *no* values any longer

[17] Albert Camus in *The Rebel* describes how both these formulations are expressed in the late Nietzsche.

[18] *After Auschwitz* (New York and Indianapolis: The Bobbs-Merrill Co., Inc., 1966), p. 20.

derive from Him—when God is oversentimentalized into the great mother who nourishes and sustains, loves and forgives, and is all *source*. God is father only when God asks and requires, when God is authority and moral judgment.

This is the center of the vitality of "the old theistic Father-God," as Rubenstein calls him, who refuses to die even for the petulant radical theologian who resents His absence or His failure to afford protection. When He is defined as "the focus of ultimate concern," His value-making and authority are what is affirmed. "He is the infinite measure against which we can see our own limited finite lives in proper perspective," Rubenstein writes. "Before God it is difficult for us to elevate the trivial to the central in our lives." Denying that God is "motive or active power," he nonetheless declares as paradoxical truth that "He shatters and makes transparent the patent unreality of every false and inauthentic standard" for He is "the ultimate measure of human truth and human potentiality."[19]

Is this then the effect of viewing God as "holy Nothingness"? If so, "nothingness" must be a dark metaphor. *"Nothingness" cannot be a measure unless nonexistence is supreme value,* as it is for the life-denying mysticisms of both East and West.

God as the source of demand is *life-affirming*. In our Jewish High Holy Day liturgy, we know Him as "the King who delights in life" just as we define our own roles as His co-workers laboring to "close iniquity's mouth" and to vanquish wickedness and arrogance among men. It is here that God is our ultimate measure, for it is *this world* that is our primary concern. God demands justice and love and the establishment of *kedusha* in *this world* as our chief goal—not the achievement of other-worldly salvation or an escape into a *nirvana* of emancipation from life, but the establishment of God's Kingship on earth.[20]

The vitality of this Father-God is such that Rubenstein is un-

[19] *After Auschwitz*, pp. 238, 240.
[20] See *The Authorized Daily Prayer Book*, ed. Joseph H. Hertz (New York: Bloch Publishing Company, 1959), pp. 895–899.

willing to let Him go. In a world in which God is dead, "a world without restraints," he confesses, nothing is left but an "ineradicable stench," and "the final lesson may very well be that there is more realistic pleasure in the disciplines and norms of the Living God than in all the freedoms of the Dead God." [21]

Recognizing that these "disciplines and norms" are no longer the dynamic determinants of the choices of men and nations, we may be led to condemn *man's* turning away rather than to proclaim *God's* death. We may be led to announce the need for a new affirmation of God's demands as written into the very constitution of reality—of all-that-is—rather than to a denial of the ontological status of our absolutes.

Anything less will make of our values only the satisfaction of our "wants" or will lead us to the conclusion of the axiologists that a "thing is good when it fulfills its own concept." Then we would have to face, bleakly, the idea that our "humanistic values" have no sanction. This is what actually would happen in society when "everything goes"—the only tests of goodness being whether or not our "wants" are satisfied, or whether or not the thing works.

When values are not simply the satisfaction of a "want" but are the propulsive power of an "ought," when they are the normative values that control decision-making and judgment, they imply the existence of a prior commitment. The essential nature of this relationship between value and the enduring demand to which we must bring a commitment, is recognized by at least one contemporary value-philosopher. Henry Margenau tells us that values are arbitrary choices unless they are related to "command." For example, life has no "value" to a person who is earnestly committed to its destruction, as in war. But Margenau says, "If you are committed to the prior maxim expressed in the Decalogue 'Thou shalt not kill' then the value of life follows as a theorem follows from a postulate." So it is with honesty, veracity, friendship, love of mankind, and every other ideal.

[21] *After Auschwitz,* pp. 36, 44.

They receive their "value" from a command, a directive to which the individual is committed.[22]

This "value-command" is validated in the life-experience of the group that affirms it, Margenau adds, just as scientific propositions are verified by testing and application. The analogy is effective in that both the scientific proposition and the value-command are initially founded upon intuitive response to experience. It falls short, however, in that the scientific proposition, if successfully tested, remains until disproved and requires no renewal of the initial hypothesis. The value-command is neither validated nor does it even function persistently within the experience of the group unless the commitment to it is continually renewed.

When we view the value-command in this light, we come very close to that central Jewish concept of an instrument that makes the Covenant-relationship function in the world—an instrument known in Hebrew as *mitzvah*.

Mitzvah is a reciprocal, two-sided term. It means the demand of God and the response of mankind. It is that which God asks of us and that which we do, in answer to that demand. *Mitzvah* is the vessel that gives form and substance to the teachings of the Covenant. "For the mitzvah is a lamp and the Torah is light." [23] Just as there can be no light without the lamp, so the

---

[22] See Henry Margenau "The Scientific Basis of Value Theory," in *New Knowledge in Human Values,* ed. Abraham H. Maslow (New York: Harper & Brothers, 1959), p. 42. For the axiologist's view, see Robert Hartman, "The Science of Value," in the same volume, p. 20.

[23] Proverbs 6:23. *Mitzvah* is a noun created from the verb *tzeevoh,* which means, in its intensive form, "to direct, to charge, to command." There is reason to believe that in its simple form as *tsovah*—called the *"kal"*—it originally meant to "join together." It has in fact that meaning in rabbinic literature. (See Marcus Jastrow, *Dictionary of Targumin, Talmud,* etc., p. 1267.) *Mitzvah* is the *bond* between God and Israel. The Covenant, the *B'rit,* which expresses that bond, becomes effective only through *mitzvah.* There is reason to believe, as we examine the use of the term, that *mitzvah* originally meant the ethical injunctions of the Torah, whereas the *chukim* (cf. *"chukot hagoyim"*) were the ordinances regarding the formal *practice* of the religious life, and the *mishpatim* were the laws of equity regarding judgments to be made between man and man. (See article *"Mitzvah,"* by Irving M. Levey, in the *Universal Jewish Encyclopedia.*)

teachings, the Torah, cannot become viable without the *mitzvah,* the deed that makes possible their fulfillment.

The paradox and the core of the mystery are found just here: *mitzvah* is at one and the same time God's demand and man's response in action. "This *mitzvah* which I command thee this day," is the Divine obverse, and "it [the *mitzvah*] is very nigh unto thee, in thy mouth, and in thy heart, that thou mayest *do* it" [24] is the human reverse and looks at the same concept from man's side of the coin.

This poses a problem for liberals. Orthodox Jews have no difficulty in determining what the *mitzvah* is. What God demands is the fulfillment of 613 commandments, both negative and positive, as recorded in the Pentateuch and as seen through the spectrum of the oral tradition and its development down through the ages. For the orthodox, the codes, and the decisions of the last great "deciders" [25] in Jewish tradition, define what a Jew is expected to do. From the moment he opens his eyes in the morning to the moment he closes them at night, and to the moment that he closes them on his deathbed, his conduct is prescribed. But how do liberals discern the divine demand?

Jewish tradition records conflicting opinions about the relative importance of specific *mitzvot* in the wide variety of 613 injunctions. We are told, on the one hand, that we are not to distinguish between the performance of a seemingly "light" *mitzvah* and a seemingly "heavy" one.[26] In this point of view, they are all equally the word of God, and it is not our function to say which is more important and which is less important. And yet, Rabbi Simlai transmits the tradition that all of the 613 commandments can be reduced to one command, whether it be "Seek ye Me and live," to use the words of Amos, or "the righteous shall live by his faith," to use those of Habakkuk, or "Thou shalt love thy neighbor as thyself," the great command in Leviticus,

[24] Deuteronomy 30:14; cf. "[The performance of] a *mitzvah* generates [the performance of] a *mitzvah*." The Talmud, Tractate *Avot* IV:2.

[25] The Hebrew term is *pos'kim,* the general title of rabbinical teachers who were qualified to make decisions after the completion of the Talmud.

[26] Talmud, Tractate *Avot* II:1.

which, for Akiba, was the *"k'lal gadol sheba-Torah,"* the great inclusive principle in the Torah.[27]

Liberal Jews read Scripture not as the literal word of God, but as the work of members of the people of Israel seeking to *understand* the demand of God. Once we approach our Bible within that frame of reference, we become necessarily selective, for there are points in Scripture at which man had broken through to an understanding of the highest, whereas there are also other points that preserve primitive practices, anachronisms, or injunctions that long ago became obsolete. For example, the word in Scripture that says "Thou shalt not seethe a kid in its mother's milk" [28] is a *mitzvah* in the sense in which the 613 commandments are spoken of in Orthodoxy. But although it has lost meaning as well as force for liberals, in Orthodoxy it becomes the foundation of all those laws of *kashrut* that have to do with the separation of milk and meat dishes. Liberal Judaism puts "Thou shalt not seethe the kid in its mother's milk" on one level and puts on another level of importance and of meaningfulness the injunction of Leviticus that tells us not to harvest the corners of our fields.[29] Even though we no longer engage in the latter practice—unhappily most of us do not possess fields and do not bring in the harvest—we nevertheless can understand the ethical ideal that would have us retain the corner of our fields for the poor and needy. Here is a law that is anachronistic and yet approaches the great ideal of *tzedakah,* "righteous action," concern for those who do not possess enough of the world's material goods and who must be taken care of by those who do possess material goods in abundance.

[27] See Talmud, Tractate *Makkot* 236–24a; the *Sifra* to Leviticus 19:18; Genesis Rabba, XXIV:5 (Soncino translation XXIV:7, p. 204). The functional emphasis in Judaism is indicated in exaggerated fashion by the fact that one sage, Shim'on Ben Pazi, cited by Theodor in his note on this passage, makes Exodus 29:39 the inclusive principle: "The one lamb thou shalt offer in the morning"! Theodor says this dictum is "strange" and that he himself searched through six orders of the Talmud without finding it. It is obviously an intentional hyperbole to make the point that the punctilious fulfillment of *every* command is required.

[28] Exodus 34:26.

[29] Leviticus 19:9–10.

On an entirely different level of perennially renewed meaningfulness, we read the great commands: "Thou shalt love thy neighbor as thyself" and "thou shalt love him [the stranger] as thyself for ye were strangers in the land of Egypt." [30]

Actually, the word *mitzvah* is used in two different ways. We talk about specific *mitzvot*. We also speak of *Mitzvah* in a general sense, as enjoining upon us a certain attitude toward our fellows. Abraham Joshua Heschel makes clear this comprehensive meaning of *Mitzvah* when he quotes Rabbi Nachman of Brazlov, the Chassidic sage, as having said, "Every act done in agreement with the will of God is *Mitzvah*.[31] George Foot Moore, the Christian expert on the thinking of our rabbis of the first and second centuries, says that the word *mitzvah* is most frequently used as meaning not a specific commandment, but any *particular* opportunity "to fulfill the comprehensive duty of men to their fellows.[32] Thus to do a *mitzvah* is to act in accord with God's will, in accord with God's demand upon mankind, and we are therefore under obligation to seek to hear the divine address.

As a modern rabbi and a liberal Jew, I cannot hear the demand of the Eternal in questions of ritual. But I can sense the address of Ultimate Reality in the command to love my neighbor, to do justly, to be concerned about the stranger, for they contain values that we can associate with that which *endures*.

Ritual has an aesthetic function: to beautify; it has a dramatic function: to make living and real the values and ideals that have come down to us. It has importance to the continuity of a people's tradition and faith. But ritual is not the demand of God. We may shape our folkways, revise our music, change our prayers, eliminate customs, and add other and new customs, *because* they are folkways; but *Mitzvah* must be something that does not change. Ritual, with its folk associations, its customs, music,

---

[30] Leviticus 19:18, 34.

[31] Abraham Joshua Heschel, *God in Search of Man* (Philadelphia: Jewish Publication Society, 1956), p. 361. (The entire section from p. 352 to p. 363 will repay careful reading. We have departed from Heschel only in our non-Orthodox distinction between ritual and what we have called enduring demand and in finding *Mitzvah* only in the latter.)

[32] *Judaism*, II, 171.

and symbols, is the carrier and preserver of values, the structural framework. But *Mitzvah*, the sense of divine demand issuing in moral and spiritual values, is the enduring essence to which the structure testifies.

This distinction is made by the prophets of Israel as far back as the eighth century B.C.E. When Amos proclaimed the words, "I hate, I despise your feasts and I will take no delight in your solemn assemblies . . . but let justice well up as waters and righteousness as a mighty stream," [33] he was making a distinction between formal adherence to practices of ritual observance and the response to the great demand of God. When Isaiah cried out, "To what purpose is the multitude of your sacrifices unto Me? . . . Who hath required this at your hand, to trample My courts? . . . Cease to do evil, learn to do well, seek justice, relieve the oppressed," [34] and when Micah summarized God's demand, "Wherewith shall I come before the Lord, and bow myself before God on high? Shall I come before Him with burnt-offerings. . . . Will the Lord be pleased with thousands of rams, with ten thousand rivers of oil? . . . It hath been told thee, O man, what is good and what the Lord doth require of thee— only to do justly and to love mercy and to walk humbly with thy God" [35] they were both seeking to give expression to the inner meaning of *Mitzvah*. They were saying that formal ritual observance is not necessarily the expression of God's will, and hence not necessarily *Mitzvah*, the divine demand.

Making *Mitzvah* equivalent to the hearing of the Divine address as well as the response to that address has the defect of investing the individual with ultimate authority as to what is *Mitzvah* and what is not *Mitzvah*. This is the dilemma that Martin Buber confronted.[36] It is a dilemma that liberalism cannot escape without relinquishing its commitment to the right of decision as the supreme right of the individual soul. But the awesomeness of this existential responsibility and its aloneness

33 Amos 5:21–24.
34 Isaiah 1:11–17.
35 Micah 6:6–8.
36 See above, Chapter X (p. 145).

are mitigated when one stands in the midst of the covenant community. Then he is bidden to hear the *Mitzvah* as an informed and committed individual within the informed and committed community. It is in the experience of that community that the "commands" that give rise to "values" are generated. Anyone who identifies himself with that community preserves and develops its special value-stance and its distinctive approach to relationship. He does not, however, relinquish his right to respond directly to the divine demand as it speaks to him, nor need he lose it in the midst of a complicated system of regulations.

Mitzvah is presented in this direct sense in Deuteronomy: [37] By Biblical definition it is that which is close to us (*ki karov aylecha*) and within our capacity (*lo ba-shamayim hi*) and on which we are obliged to act (*la-asoto*). *Mitzvah* therefore speaks differently to us than it did to our great-great-grandfather. Cut off from the larger world, he retained the ideal of mankind's ultimate perfection, in his liturgy, in his aspirations, and in his obligation under the covenant *l'takayn olam*—"to perfect the world." But the only task that was within his *capacity* as a Jew was to be faithful, to observe the 613 *mitzvot* and to practice *kiddush hashem* in his relationship to the world. He prayed for the time when the just would exult and wickedness would vanish, when God would be King over the earth; but he did not have to *do* anything about it. The quarrels among kings and princes, the violence and the cruelty, the servitude of the peasants, were all part of "the world of the Gentiles"—he had no access to it. Even when he recognized that the most stringent troubles were those that affected *both* Israel and the world, he could not but feel that the only action required of him was personal witness and prayer.

We, in contrast to our great-grandfathers, are *part* of the larger world. This is the precious and unhappy result of emancipation. We cannot say "What's Vietnam to me or I to Vietnam?" We are participants, in destiny and in responsibility, with all men. Most of us no longer observe the 613 commandments

[37] Deuteronomy 30:11–14.

and cannot even pretend to be building God's Kingdom by the faithful witness of personal discipline. For us, the demand of God that challenges us to compassion and to respect for the divine image in every fellow man must as *Mitzvah* eventuate in the *mitzvah* that is performance: *action in* the world in behalf of human rights, justice, and peace.

This conception of the role of *Mitzvah* is not alien to our tradition. The Midrash tells us that "*the mitzvot* were given to Israel in order to purify mankind." [38] These particular and specific commands were given for a universal purpose.

It may be said by the contemporary reductionist that, in developing this concept of *Mitzvah* and in claiming to *experience* a demand that is made upon us, we are simply projecting our own values on a universe which is in reality indifferent to whether we love or hate, whether we destroy ourselves or whether we survive. But that view itself could be characterized as a projection of man's loneliness and despair upon the universe. We have already pointed to the findings of scientific thinkers like Teilhard de Chardin, who testify to increasing coherence, increasing harmony, and the ever greater refinement of consciousness as constituting the central thrust of cosmic evolution. Other testimony can be drawn, however, from aspects of experience far more accessible to the average man. It lies in what is popularly called "conscience" and in actual universal recognition of what is good and what is evil. This is why what our American founding fathers called "a decent respect for the opinions of mankind" is a reliable guide to the good.

It would be an unspeakable validation of nihilism, as well as a shattering blow to our faith in democracy, if we did not believe that *most* men must acknowledge either openly or "in their innermost beings" that Hitlerism was evil incarnate. They acknowledge this by their guilt and their rationalizations even when they support evil. Experience testifies to a conflict between an inclination to good and an inclination to evil. When men open themselves to the divine address they strengthen the inclination to good. When men deny God by making power or the exaltation

[38] Leviticus Rabba, XIII:3 (Soncino translation, p. 166).

of the Self at the expense of the Other their supreme goals, evil triumphs.

What Freud saw as a conflict between *id* and *superego,* rabbinic tradition saw as a conflict between a *yetser tov* and a *yetser ra,* two basic natures in man.[39] The *yetser ra,* frequently personalized in folklore and legend, has an essential role to play in life. Without it, no man would marry or build a house—indeed, no chicken would lay an egg.[40] It is the *libido,* without which life would be devoid of color and dynamism, but which, if given full license, could return human life to the level of the animals.

But man, the decisive agent in the determination of good and evil, cannot use this nature of things to exculpate himself from responsibility for his actions. The Talmud pictures Job as having tried this rationalization: "Sovereign of the Universe, Thou hast created the ox with cloven hoofs and Thou hast created the ass with whole hoofs. . . . Thou hast created righteous men and Thou hast created wicked men and who can prevent Thee?" They interpret the answer of Eliphaz, "Yea, Thou doest away with fear and impairest devotion before God" [41] as meaning that even though evil is present in our world we have been given an antidote to evil—the Torah, God's teachings, the gift of the *mitzvot,* God's demands.[42]

Man is obliged to present himself to the divine demand—the demand that he affirm life and conquer evil. This view of man's responsibility helps us when we struggle with the age-old problem of evil—the "impossible problem," as John Stuart Mill named it.[43] This is the problem that rises with unprecedented force to trouble contemporary religious thinkers because the power of evil has now reached unprecedented heights. Evil is

[39] The word *"yetser"* comes from the root meaning "to create" and thus means man's basic endowment. The *yetser ra* is the evil component of man's endowment; the *yetser tov* is the good.

[40] Genesis Rabba, IX:7 (Soncino translation, p. 68). Talmud, Tractate *Yoma* 69b (Soncino translation, p. 328).

[41] Job 15:4.

[42] Talmud, Tractate *Baba Batra* 16a (Soncino translation, p. 80).

[43] John Stuart Mill, "Essay on Theism," in *Essays on Politics and Culture,* ed. Gertrude Himmelfarb (New York: Doubleday & Company, 1962), Part II, p. 447. Mill concludes that God is not omnipotent.

now abetted by technology. Where previous ages were limited to sword and flame or torture devices designed to rack one individual at a time, Adolf Hitler had access both to perfected extermination gases and assembly-line procedures.

For Jewish thinkers, Auschwitz has become the symbol of the final breaking point—for Auschwitz was the death camp that the Nazis established at the small town of that name, some thirty miles west of Kraków, and known in Polish as Oświecim. This was the camp at which the "processing" of Jews was perfected so that thousands each day could be passed through its four modern gas chambers into its modern crematoriums. Only some 90 per cent of the almost 2,000,000 Jews brought to that camp were put through the "process." The other 10 per cent were killed more slowly by starvation, inhuman treatment, and disease.

Auschwitz, therefore, stands for the entire Nazi holocaust in our minds. It represents the final breaking point. It is specifically so to a death-of-God theologian like Rubenstein, who says that if he believed in the Biblical God he would have to believe that God *willed* the destruction of the 6,000,000 Jews who were systematically done to death in the Hitler program.[44]

But Auschwitz is a new phenomenon only in a quantitative and technological sense. One must say this with care, with reverence for life, with respect for those who died—and with bitterness. But it is true. The prophet Habakkuk more than two millennia ago, testified to the perennial presence of the unaccountable triumph of injustice:

. . . I cry out unto Thee of violence, and Thou wilt not save . . .
For the wicked doth beset the righteous; . . .
Wherefore lookest Thou, when they deal treacherously,
And holdest Thy peace when the wicked swalloweth up
The man that is more righteous than he.[45]

Even men who put on the garb of Christian fidelity and set out on the Crusades showed the face of evil.

A leading Jewish historian writes:

[44] *After Auschwitz*, p. 46.
[45] Habakkuk 1:2, 4, 13.

It seemed to the Crusaders preposterous to journey afar to fight the infidel while leaving behind them untouched the archinfidels of all time, who were actually responsible for the Crucifixion—all the more so if murder might result in canceling their debts or help to equip them for their journey. Accordingly, the First Crusade of 1096 gave the signal for a series of sanguinary onslaughts on the Jews of the Rhineland . . . Thereafter massacre became the accompaniment of each Crusade . . . It was from the period of the Crusades that the Jews became the true Niobe of nations, ever having to bewail the slaughter of helpless children.[46]

In the year 1298 alone, over 100,000 Jews were murdered in Germany and Austria.[47] When the Black Plague struck Europe, it became a pretext for massacres in which more than 200,000 Jews were done to death.[48] The year 1648 lives in the history of Jewish tragedy as a year in which sadistic violence reached a peak that was not exceeded until the holocaust of our own day, for that was the year in which the Cossack hordes of Chmielnitzki swept through the pale of Jewish settlement pillaging, raping, and slaughtering the innocent in village after village.[49]

The cry of the Psalmist, "For Thy sake are we slaughtered all the day," [50] was echoed by generation after generation. These were the martyrs who died *al kiddush hashem*.[51] For they would not accept the easy escape of baptism. It should be repeated that in our era the Jews were offered no alternative to the death that the "master race" had decreed for them.

The gory recital up to this point has been a subjective and particularistic view of the depravity of man. Jews were certainly

[46] Cecil Roth, "The European Age in Jewish History," in *The Jews: Their History, Culture, and Religion,* ed. Louis Finkelstein (Philadelphia: Jewish Publication Society, 1949), I, 224–225; see also p. 233.

[47] See article "Rindfleisch," in *Universal Jewish Encyclopedia.*

[48] See Jacob R. Marcus, *The Jew in the Medieval World* (Cincinnati: Union of American Hebrew Congregations, 1938), pp. 43–48.

[49] See S. M. Dubnow, *The History of the Jews in Russia and Poland* (Philadelphia: Jewish Publication Society, 1916), I, 144 ff., where unbelievable cruelties are described.

[50] Psalm 44:23.

[51] See above, Chapter Nine (p. 137).

not the only victims of man's capacity for bestiality. The cruelty of Genghis Khan is more than legendary. His westward sweep in the thirteenth century left a trail of blood that linked his terror with that of his fifth-century predecessor, Attila, who had made the name "Hun" the synonym, for the ages, of murderous scorn for the image of God.[52]

The quantitative aspect of human evil is increasing only because man has more efficient instruments at his disposal. Some American patriots are horrified when the flaming-death agonies of more than 78,000 noncombatant men, women, and children at Hiroshima and of many thousands more at Nagasaki are brought within this frame of reference. The curse of technology is that the stakes are higher; but the responsibility of decision is the same. The turning away from the divine demand is no less real when it is supported by expediency or by rationalization. Evil has always been able to wear the cloak of good. Men can persuasively claim that they are loyal to a higher cause or that they are "obeying orders." Whether it is an Adolf Eichmann who does so, or the unhappy pilot of the *Enola Gay,* or the luckless individual who will feel compelled to push the button tomorrow, the result is mass destruction of the innocent.

The discovery of thermonuclear instruments for destruction—and man's newborn capacity to wipe himself out—not only makes new weapons available to the powers of evil, but also brings with it the capacity for new excuses, and thus sharpens man's decision-making responsibility. It is a responsibility that cannot be sloughed off by playing the numbers game (let the bomb take 100,000 of "theirs" if it will spare 200,000 of "ours"). The doomsday devices unite us into one mankind and, in a deeper sense than ever before, through the confrontation of common death, make all men kin. The rabbinic adage that "he

[52] "For a whole week the Mongols ceased not to kill, burn and destroy [at Herat], and 1,600,000 are said to have been massacred within the walls." This one instance of characteristic cruelty is cited by Sir Robert K. Douglas, in his article, "Jenghis Khan," *Encyclopaedia Britannica,* 11th ed., Vol. XV, p. 317b. See also the article by Thomas Hodgkin, "Attila," in Vol. II, p. 885.

who destroys one life has it accounted to him as if he had destroyed the entire world" [53] takes on grim, new meaning.

This does give the problem of evil new dimensions, but it does not change its essential nature. The "impossible" antinomy was there before Auschwitz. The phrase "God willed the death of the six-million" must be gall in the mouth of any sensitive modern. But I cannot with less distaste say that God "willed" the murderous acts of ancient conquerors, that God "willed" the Chmielnitzski massacres, or that God "willed" Guernica or Dresden or Hiroshima. Indeed, the word "will" in this connection is an anthropomorphism that supports an almost blasphemous ingenuousness. If this use of "will" applies to God, it cannot be a "will" that is in any sense accessible to the human intellect. When the phrase "it was God's will" is used in pious naïveté, it is tantamount to saying no more than "that's the way it was."

It may be said in rejoinder that "God's demand" is just as anthropomorphic a phrase as "God's will." This is so, except for the significant distinction that, when I say I experience God's demand, I describe something that happens in *me*—that I have a sense of something being *required* or asked of me.

Rejecting the idea that God "willed" the death camps means rejecting what is technically known in theology as the doctrine of special providence (as opposed to general providence). It means that we have no experience of God "willing" the fate of individual men, rewarding them or punishing them in accordance with their conduct, or being responsible for human suffering. To say that in doing so we are rejecting the "Biblical God" means nothing, for, as we have already said [54] many different conceptions of God are present in the Bible, including a "Biblical God" who admitted to having made a mistake in creating man and proceeded to correct it by wiping out mankind in a flood.[55]

---

[53] *The Mishnah, Sanhedrin* IV:5 (Danby translation, p. 388, and footnote thereto). The favored reading omits the words, "of Israel," as we do here.

[54] See above, Chapter Four (pp. 63–64).

[55] Gabriel Vahanian says (*Wait Without Idols* [New York: George Braziller, 1964], p. xii): "The Bible speaks of God in terms of a world

If this is the "Biblical God," it is a concept that has been rejected by scores of thinkers within the normative tradition, not the least among them Maimonides, who limits his special providence to "the individuals belonging to the human species" and not "in an equal manner over all the individuals of the human species, but providence is graded as their human perfection is graded." [56] Here he is struggling to avoid the "disgraceful" results and the incongruities that, he said, flow from the thinking of that school of Islamic thought known as the *Mu'tazila,* who held that God "has knowledge of the falling of this particular leaf and of the creeping of this particular ant." But Maimonides knows that this limitation that he has boldly made has not solved the problem of evil, and his final refuge is the Jobian affirmation that the ways of God are beyond human understanding.

The problem of evil cannot be solved as it stands—something has to give. What usually does give is some aspect of divine omnipotence. In traditional terms, human freedom is a divinely generous act of self-limitation. It attributes no defect to God to say that He "knows" things as they are. For John Stuart Mill, the defect inheres in the nature of the material—an echo of Leibnitz' assertion that *anything* created is thereby contingent and must be imperfect. William James sets forth a variant of this "solution" in an essay, "The Dilemma of Determinism":

> If you allow Him possibilities as well as actualities to the universe, and to carry on His own thinking in these two categories just as we do ours, chance may be there uncontrolled even by Him, and the course of the universe be really ambiguous, yet the end of all things may be just what He intended it from all eternity.[57]

---

view to which it also adheres in other respects. It is consistent within itself." This generalization, although a widely held preconception, is untrue. Compare the God of Judges 5 and Exodus 15 with the God of Isaiah and Leviticus 19.

[56] Maimonides, *The Guide For the Perplexed,* Part III, Chapters 17 and 18 (Pines translation, pp. 471 and 475).

[57] William James, *The Will to Believe and Other Essays in Popular Philosophy* (New York: Longmans, Green and Company, 1898), pp. 180 f.

To this, James appends his engaging analogy of the master chess player who, although he is unable to foresee any specific actual move of his opponent, knows all the possibilities and is certain of the final checkmate. Traditional philosophy would call this accepting the idea of contingency as *part* of Divine foreknowledge. It means recognizing that there can be no morality, no achievement, without struggle. "To realize the moral ideal *per saltum,* by an act of omnipotence, would be to annihilate it," says A. B. Bruce.[58]

There is an equanimity, it must be admitted, about these late nineteenth-century, pre-Auschwitz thinkers that has a quaint and unrealistic ring when measured against the monstrosities of our time. We must paraphrase James by saying that *evil* is there— gargantuan evil—uncontrolled by Him. We cannot pretend to know why—we can only cling stubbornly to the conviction that there *is* meaning—*lam'rot hakol,* in spite of everything. In the cosmic scope that new knowledge brings to *hashgacha k'lalit*— the *over-all* divine plan—there is that which is demanded of *us.*

As a Jew who places himself within the covenant community, I must interpret my responsibility as it is defined by the covenant task—to battle evil and to perfect the world. I accept as allies all who labor for the same end, whether they enter the covenant community or not, whether they speak of God or not. But as I hear it, the greater the evil, the more insistent and the more intense, even to the point of anguish, is the demand.

"After the death camps," says Richard Rubenstein, "the doctrine of Israel's election is . . . a thoroughly distasteful pill to swallow." [59] This is so if the "election" means that God is protector and "Guardian of Israel," if the election of Israel means "a special religious destiny." [60] But it is not so if election means a special task rather than special privilege. The prophet who wrote "You only have I known . . ." also warns us that we have

[58] A. B. Bruce, in his Gifford Lectures, *The Providential Order of the World* (New York: Charles Scribner's Sons, 1897), p. 125.

[59] *After Auschwitz,* p. 69.

[60] *After Auschwitz,* p. 74.

no greater claim on God than have the other peoples of the earth.[61]

This fact of experience is given its most dramatic and touching expression by the voice of an unnamed prophet who spoke out of the torment of having witnessed destruction and gone into exile. Personalized as the "servant," the people of Israel are to persist despite their weakness—a weakness unequal to the task of breaking even a bruised reed or of quenching even a dimly burning wick—until they "have set the right in the earth." This the "servant" is to do despite ugliness and pain and disease, despite being wounded and crushed by the wickedness of men.[62]

In this prophetic portion and in the historic experience of the Jews, which it immortalizes, it becomes clear that suffering for an ideal—even suffering monumentally and dying for an ideal—is not an unassimilable concept in Jewish thought. Giving one's life for an ideal is *kiddush hashem:* testimony to the compelling power of the divine demand.

As I cannot say that God "willed" the death of the 6,000,000, so I certainly cannot "praise Him for their death." [63] This to me is a repelling, blasphemous idea. But I cannot withdraw from the 6,000,000 the dignity that lies in recognition that there existed among them a willingness to die in fulfillment of a distinctive role. That thousands fought with incredible courage and with the certainty of the futility of resistance is no myth.[64] That thousands marched to the freight cars that were to carry them into Hell with the *"Ani Ma-amin"* [65] on their lips is also no myth. The very words of the song demonstrate that they knew their destination and that this pronouncement in music,

[61] Amos 3:2, 9:7.

[62] Isaiah 42:1–9; 52:13–15; 53. These are, of course, the "suffering servant" passages, revered in Christianity as a description of Jesus in his messianic role, but speaking originally to the actuality of Israel in its covenant role.

[63] *After Auschwitz,* p. 70.

[64] See Yuri Suhl, *They Fought Back* (New York: Crown Publishers, Inc., 1967).

[65] "I believe," or better, "I affirm."

like the other songs of the Jewish partisans, was an act of defiance. The words—taken from the Maimonidean thirteen principles that have become part of synagogue liturgy—are:

I affirm, with unbroken firmness, that the Messiah will come. And even though He tarries, even so, I affirm it.[66]

Theology—even the nontheology of the radicals—is not always coextensive with life. Men persist in holding fast to a relationship with that which is greater than Self, even in the midst of difficulties that increase to the breaking point the tension in the classical contradictions of cognitive analysis. We have said that Hitler's victims were offered no alternative. This is not wholly so. They had the alternative of dying as cravens, of cursing God and their identity. All the evidence says that in overwhelming numbers they died with dignity. As for the earlier generations who were offered the Cross as a way out, who by simple conversion could have been given the alternative of life, it can be said that the thousands upons thousands of victims of the Crusades in central or western Europe and of the pogroms in the East went to horrible deaths without sacrificing their integrity.

The relationship in extremity is frequently one of Promethean dimensions. Like the ancient, tortured Titan chained to his rock and defying the Olympians, those about to die manifest a stubbornness tinged with resentment and protest. The mood is that of Job: "Let Him slay me—I have no hope—but I will defend my actions to His face." "Till I die I will not put away my integrity from me." [67] This is a saving grace inherent in Jewish realism. We feel free to argue with God, to shake a fist at the Almighty.

One prized example of this temperament is widely known because it is imbedded in a song popular in the repertories of celebrated singers. It is the *Kaddish* of the eighteenth-century

[66] The song abbreviates, with unmistakable emphasis, the Maimonidean original, which says: "Even though he tarry even so I shall wait for Him, every day, that He may come."

[67] Job 13:15 (reading the text as written, not as traditionally received), and Job 27:5.

Chassidic Rebbe, Levi Yitzchok of Berdichev. Called a *"Din Torah mit Gott,"* a civil case against God, it represents Levi Yitzchok as challenging God with unfairness to Israel and then, threatening not to move from his place until there is an end to Jewish suffering, lapsing into the great doxology of the Jewish liturgy.

A kind of blessed stubbornness shows itself again and again in the traditional Jewish sources. The problem of evil is met with an *emunah*—a persistence in relationship [68]—that faces reality without abandoning covenant loyalty. The death of those pre-eminent second-century teachers who were martyred in the Hadrianic persecutions must have been a severe blow to their disciples. The teachers of the following century recorded their protest by imagining Moses being shown the future and marveling at the dedicated scholarship of Akiba ben Joseph, who was destined to be flayed alive by the Hadrianic torturers:

> Then said Moses, "Lord of the Universe, Thou hast shown me his Torah, Show me his reward." "Turn thee round," said He; and Moses turned round and saw them weighing out his [Akiba's] flesh at the market-stalls. "Lord of the Universe," cried Moses, "such Torah, and such a reward?" He replied, "Be silent, for such is My decree." [69]

The tradition also records that Akiba in the moment of his excruciating death told his disciples that he then understood for the first time what it meant to love God with all one's "soul"![70]

The rabbinic teachers were not unaware of the existential absurdities that trouble modern thinkers. They possessed a supreme gift for paradox, firmly grasping *both* horns of every spiritual dilemma. That gift is revealingly present in the dry Talmudic comment on the disastrous defeat at Betar that ended the revolt against Hadrian. The fortress Betar was the scene of

---

[68] See above, Chapter Eleven (p. 160).

[69] Talmud, Tractate *Menachot* 29b (Soncino translation, p. 190). The words translated "such is My decree" are literally "so it has arisen in thought before Me," which may suggest a limitation of Divine power but which I read as meaning nothing more than "That's the way it is."

[70] *Berachot* 61b (Soncino translation, p. 386).

the last stand in the rebellion led by Bar Kochba. It held out
for a year, until every last defender was dead. And the Talmud
records:

> On the very day on which the slain of Betar were buried [the
> rabbinic leaders of the academy] in Yavneh established [in the
> liturgy for the grace after meals] the saying of the blessing [that
> describes God as] "He who is good and does good to all." [71]

The paradox arises out of the experiences of life. It is a fact
that evil triumphs again and again; it is a fact that God is experienced by men as compassionate and good. The paradox is
resolved when we confront God as the source of demand. The
father who expects much of his son may for the sake of his son
refrain from interfering in his life and at the same time weep
for his son's suffering. The Midrash to Lamentations, a fourth-
century collection of sermonic materials and discourses on the
Biblical book of that title, conceives of God as weeping for the
sufferings of men.[72] And I have no doubt that the metaphor
points to a profound truth—that there is sympathy at the heart
of the universe. In this sense, while I cannot say that God
"willed" Auschwitz, I can say that God "wept" over Auschwitz.

Because men are responsible agents and free deciders, the
architects of Auschwitz were free to turn their backs on God
and to reject the divine demand, the demand that the good made
upon them. To say that they turned away from the ultimate
values that are somehow written into the very constitution of
the universe and direct its unfolding, is an act of faith. It is a
faith that the same Ultimate which is the ground of all-that-is,
and which orders and unifies all-that-is, also infuses purpose
and meaning into all-that-is. In some way hidden to our intel-
lects, but consonant with what we know, and clear to the eye of
faith, there are in that Ultimate, properties that are akin to
harmony and to love, which must contain sympathy for the very
men on whom these ultimate values make their demands: Sym-

---

[71] *Berachot* 48b (Soncino translation, p. 292).
[72] Midrash Rabba to Lamentations 1:16, Paragraphs 45–51 (Soncino
translation, pp. 124–135).

pathy for their strivings, sympathy for their sufferings, sympathy for justice, brotherhood, and peace.

This conviction about the nature of things is supported by the limited number of alternative possibilities. Either the universe is sympathetic to man's strivings, or it is indifferent, or it is antagonistic. Of course, it may be no one of these three, but some peculiar *mélange* totally foreign to our understanding. An agnostic position is an admissable response to these alternatives: "I do not know whether these alternatives exhaust the possibilities inherent in the totality of being. It is fruitless to discuss it, and I will just do the best I can with what is given to me."

This seems to me a sterile position. Most men feel forced to decide and, in actuality, do decide that the universe is either indifferent, or antagonistic, or sympathetic—manifesting their decisions in their temperament, in the way in which they relate to life.

To affirm that the universe is indifferent is to ignore the evidences of purposiveness and coherence that are present in the cosmos. Indifference means chance—things will fall where they happen to fall. But if modern science has any relevance to our problem, it lies in the profound new support that, as we have shown,[73] it has given to the old argument from design.

To believe that the universe is antagonistic is to fall into a position wholly untenable for modern man, for it would mean that whatever has been accomplished by man in his painful climb through the millennia, his physical evolution and intellectual achievement, his wresting of secrets from the natural world, his capacity for love and benevolence, his creativity in art and in technique, are all a conquest over unimaginable odds, a defeat, so to speak, of a malign God.

The sympathy that we affirm as our only remaining possibility is present within a total complex inaccessible to the intellect. It is not the kind of sympathy that encourages our neurotic dependence upon it. It is rather an aspect of the insistent demand of the universe that the harmony toward which it moves be

[73] See above, Chapter Six (pp. 93–95); Chapter Seven (p. 107); see also below, Chapter Twelve (pp. 186, 195).

fulfilled. It is the refusal of that demand that brings grim consequences for man.

It is a sympathy that permits relationship, that enables man to enter into "partnership" with God. When we confront God not as the source of love of a kind that has "no bones at all" but as the God of demand who holds the plumb line of eternal righteousness in His hand, we may feel compelled to enter into alliance with His purposes—to be *"m'shutaf,"* joined to God in fighting evil. This stance makes a world of difference in our reactions.

In this stance, I cannot believe that the great task of the God of all the galaxies and of all-that-is is to wrap me in an envelope of love and kindness and to take care of *me*. This is so, even though I believe that love and coherence and harmony are written into the constitution of the universe and that the thrust of cosmic evolution is toward greater love, greater harmony, and greater justice. This outlook, in its insistence that there is meaning and purpose in the whole, is an affirmation of general providence, but, in its recognition that chance, disorder, and error are also part of what we experience, it entails a rejection of special providence.

Most people who affirm that God lives have not emancipated themselves from the juvenile notion that the chief function of God is to take care of them. This is why they reject God or question God when they run into sorrow, frustration, or bereavement. I have put to my teen-age and adult classes the question, "What do you think of, when you think about the word 'God'?" Some 70 per cent of them respond with notions of protection, solace, and comfort. They are scarcely aware of the self-centered, infantile enormity of their response: "God is for *me;* to take care of me, coddle me, see to it that I am guarded against the roughness and difficulty of life." Inevitably, this view brings shattering disappointment. It is asking the impossible of the universe. Life is contingency and risk; it is marked by rigor and the built-in frustrations of mortality. We cannot avoid imperfection, failure, and death.

When the individual who has clung to this God of selfish

sentimentalism meets these inevitabilities, his cry is, "Why did God do this to me? Why did God withdraw His love and suddenly stop protecting and comforting me?" But when our relationship to God is that of Covenant responsibility, when God is the guarantor of value and the source of demand, then the confrontation of evil elicits not the plaintive "Why did God do this?" but rather "What does God ask of me?" In this human situation of injustice, of suffering, of loss, even of absurdity, "What doth the Lord require?"

When we confront God as the source of demand, we concentrate our attention on this world in which we live. Striving to place ourselves within all that moves to fulfill His purposes, we find that there is in the universe that which aids and supports us. We may still say and feel that "God is a very present help in trouble" (Psalm 46:1)—not in a disabling overconcern with "*my* salvation" or "*my* peace of mind," but in a bolstering courage and will to participate in perfecting the world and bringing about the redemption of all mankind.

The religion of demand is not vulnerable, as is the religion of beyond, to the blows of historical change or the pressures of advancing knowledge. The essential human situation of quest for perfection in relationship remains unchanged. James Darmesteter, an eminent French Orientalist, said this of Judaism a half-century ago:

> In this great downfall of mythical religion, the crash of which fills our age, Judaism, such as the centuries have made it, has had the least to suffer and the least to fear, because its miracles and its rites constitute no essential and integral part of it.[74]

Darmesteter was able to say this because, for him, Judaism was summed up in the messianic ideal and the ethical demand. These are, indeed, supremely precious ingredients. They are the twin pillars of an outlook that organizes our experience and sets our goals while it neither defies reason nor dwindles into un-

[74] "An Essay on the History of the Jews," in *Selected Essays of James Darmesteter,* trans. Helen B. Jastrow (Boston and New York: Houghton, Mifflin and Co., 1895), p. 273.

poetic sterility. They are the symbols of an indestructible "No" to philosophies of despair and an everlasting "Yes" to the challenge of human fulfillment. They are the eternal context of that persistence and that striving within which we are able to proclaim that God lives.

CHAPTER TWELVE

MODERN MAN NEEDS GOD

I once read an anecdote told of Robert G. Ingersoll, the late nineteenth-century lawyer and rhetorician who became famous for his attacks on religion and his lectures denying God's existence, and of his friend and older contemporary, Henry Ward Beecher, the great Congregational preacher. Ingersoll is said to have been visiting in Beecher's study at Plymouth Church in Brooklyn, where he admired a beautifully and intricately made celestial globe. "Henry, that's magnificent," said Ingersoll. "Who made it?" Beecher looked at him with a twinkle. "Why, Robert, nobody made it," he answered. "It just happened."

Like the old watchmaker analogy, this story has an archaic and anthropomorphic ring today, but it does point to an aspect of our concern that is still meaningful. Affirming that God is dead, when it means a defense of atheism rather than a cultural evaluation, is an expression of conviction, a statement of belief. But to say that the ordered universe in which we live is without meaning, that its coherence and purposiveness just happened, requires a greater measure of credulity—a far greater "leap of faith"—than is needed for the affirmation of an ordering power.

The "argument from design" has not lost its potency when we are forced to "talk *about* God." Even though, ever since Kant, we have been unable to use it as a "demonstration" or a "proof," it is a helpful prop when we must choose between two unproven hypotheses. Indeed, the new knowledge of both galaxy and particle makes it more difficult than ever to believe that "it just happened."

The necessity to choose is built into any effort to construct a world-view that embraces all experience. Either we have faith

186

that we exist in a setting of incorrigible absurdity, or we have faith that life and striving must make sense within the total scheme.

I have tried to set forth the view that God must be found in experience—the experience of presence and of relationship as well as of demand; but I also contend that all that we know makes it reasonable for us to affirm the reality of the God whom we experience.

I have also tried to set forth a view of relationship that in the light of Buber's "I-Thou" category is free of operational limitations: when we stand in relationship in this sense we are wholly present to Him whom we confront. We do not seek to convert God into a "cosmic bellhop" with our petitions, nor do we want to make God a "gimmick" for worldly success, institutional prosperity, wealth, or peace of mind. Only in unfettered relationship do we open the door to a dialogue of address and response.

With all this, when we "talk about God" and thus enter the world of argumentation and debate, even though we are seeking the Thou that can never become an It, our affirmation that God lives does have its *instrumental* aspect. Modern man *needs* God not for His presence alone, but for what His presence can do in this world in which we live.

Modern man needs God as the guarantor of meaning. Modern man needs God as the anchorage of values, the preserver of what we esteem as essentially human.

Unless God is relevant to these needs, He is no God. There is an abiding interrelationship between the conviction that there is meaning and the sense of the divine demand. "What does it mean?" as an ultimate question is the same as "What is its purpose?" Absurdity makes no demand other than that it be accepted. Meaning makes a demand for fulfillment.

The simplest way to deny God is to live in such a way as to demonstrate that God does not count. This is the practical atheist whom we have already described, who says in effect: "He makes no demand—there is no God" (Psalm 10:4).[1] If

[1] The verb used for "makes no demand" is the same as the verb used for "require" in Micah 6:8—the Hebrew word *doresh*.

God requires nothing it is, as I have said, as if God did not exist. The converse must also be true: When one lives a life marked by respect for his fellow men, by compassion and by an active concern to promote the fulfillment of human potentiality and the creation of harmony among men, then he places himself in line with life's ultimate purposes and stands in relationship to God, whether he affirms Him or not.

The interrelationship between meaning and demand is sharply defined by that supreme *provocateur* on behalf of absurdity, Death. The fact of our mortality incites some of our most disabling psychological problems. What Erich Fromm has called the "existential dichotomy" is the most widely experienced of such problems.[2] In our youth, the world is all potentiality: there is nothing marked "impossible." We can look ahead believing that we can achieve any goal if we but take it seriously enough. In our middle years, we begin to know the truth. Our life span is limited, the years have slipped away, and all that we had hoped to do and accomplish is now frustrated by the dwindling number of remaining years and the certain end.

One way to resolve that dichotomy is to ally oneself with purposes larger than self. When, for example, one identifies himself as a member of a community that has covenanted to fulfill what it believes to be divine purpose, to perfect the world under that kingship that demands equity and harmony and reverence for life, then one is able to take the balanced view of the sage who said, "The day is short and the work is great . . . and the Employer presses . . . [but] it is not incumbent upon thee to finish the work, just as you are not free to do nothing about it. . . ."[3] If one responds according to his capacity to the divine demand, the meaning of what one is able to do, limited as it must be, is confirmed in the context of overarching meaning.

There must be many who never feel the sting of this problem, who are content with the minimal convictions they have acquired and with which they "operate" in their daily lives. The legion of

[2] See above, Chapter Two (p. 28).
[3] Talmud, Tractate *Avot* I:15 f. (Soncino translation, p. 24).

discontented is encountered by those who, like me, must seek to listen in love to the unhappinesses that are poured out across their desks day after day and week after week. One would have to be stony-hearted indeed to be free of an agonizing concern about the epidemic character of contemporary despair—a concern that, unless one lives in the isolation of a Simeon Stylites, must be a *participant* concern. No one who is part of the community of modern man, not even the listening counselor or the writer of didactic answers, can be free of the conflicts and the suffering generated by contemporary uncertainties.

One brilliant and deeply troubled young woman once put it to me in these words: "Rabbi, I don't believe in anything; and it's *killing* me!" She was, of course, speaking on behalf of hosts of her contemporaries when she protested her complete lack of conviction—even on behalf of those who are sufficiently shallow or sufficiently callous to escape the terrors that accompany such nihilism. And yet, their inability to believe in *anything* is something new under the sun. Their fathers may have rejected traditional theology, but they could not have said that they did not believe in *anything*. They "believed" in democracy, or they "believed" in the liberating power of science, or they "believed" in man. Within their turn-of-the-century humanism, they found their role. Their children, however, not only find it impossible to believe in God; they no longer have confidence in man, and they have not yet formulated a response to the new science and to the new knowledge adequate to provide them with a structure of meaning.[4]

One traditional avoidance of the existential dichotomy is no longer accessible to contemporary man, whose outlook requires that our extrapolations conform to the experienced facts: that is, the denial of the claim of mortality by positing some form of life after death in which virtue will be rewarded, wickedness requited, and all inequities made good—or in which the righteous will go "from strength to strength," continuing the process

[4] See above, Chapter Six (pp. 90–91).

of study and intellectual growth that they had initiated during their life in "this world." [5]

There is a subtle selfishness in this view. The goal of individual salvation or of a personal survival after death is not a goal that is larger than self. It is the ultimate in self-seeking, the self-proclaimed indispensability of each individual personality. Its selfishness becomes vividly apparent when the idea of life after death—usually conceived of as available only to those who are "selected" for their virtue, or "right thinking," or conformity to a specific ideology—becomes a substitute for an active concern with injustice and inequality on earth. That this kind of religion was frequently an "opiate of the masses," offering "pie in the sky" when what was needed was bread in the here and now, is a self-evident historical fact.

Even today, it is used in that sedative fashion by forces of reaction. Religion, said one rightist leader recently, must learn to perform its proper function. It must tell prospective recruits for the clergy that seminaries are not training grounds for civil rights workers. It must "concentrate on the life beyond and not on this life." [6]

The life "beyond" makes no larger waves for intelligent modern man than does the God "beyond." Whether it is used as a political instrument or as an earnest statement of one way of viewing reality, it calls for clear-minded and deeply honest analysis, such as that to which the Bishop of Woolwich subjects it.[7] God is not "beyond"; He is neither "up there" nor "out there." When we say "God" we mean that which is ultimate in all-that-is. That ultimate must make demands upon us *where we are,* and hence the insistence that *this world* be the field of our concentration. That demand may be, as it is for Bishop Robinson,[8] the prescription of love alone, or it may be all that makes rela-

---

[5] Talmud, Tractate *Berachot* 64a; cf. 17a (Soncino translation, p. 404, p. 102).

[6] Brent Bozell, speaking on Radio Station WKYC, Cleveland, Ohio, February 2, 1967.

[7] John A. T. Robinson, Bishop of Woolwich, in *Honest to God* (Philadelphia: Westminster Press, 1963).

[8] Robinson, pp. 116–118.

tionship fruitful, productive, and fulfilling, or that esteems the preciousness of life and its potentiality, and thus, as we believe, calls for the normative commands that alone create value.

The Mishnaic teacher, Rabbi Jacob, caught as he was in a world-view that admitted of a life "beyond," nevertheless gave voice to the practical emphasis that the God of demand makes necessary. Although he said, "One hour of tranquility in the world to come is more beautiful than the whole life of this world," he also said, "One hour of turning [to God] and performing good deeds in this world is more beautiful than the whole life of the world to come." [9] This is not a paradox. It is a flat rejection of the false antithesis that appears in the radio statement quoted. Life beyond or no life beyond, man's task is to concentrate on the life that is given him in this world, to *turn* and to perform the good as it is *required* of him.

A doctrine of God does not necessarily imply a doctrine of personal immortality as its corollary. Biblical religion, in which the major emphasis is on the prophetic hope of the redemption of mankind in this world, manifests no need for the idea of personal survival after death. Rabbinic thought did make use of the "theodical calculus," justifying God's ways by ideas of reward and punishment after death, but this is actually tangential to its emphasis on the fulfillment of God's demand in the here and now as a means to this-worldly redemption. Indeed, the very terms "world to come" and "future to come" are frequently used to describe a *this-worldly* salvation, a messianic time of a perfected human society.[10] This is where the emphasis of the synagogue and study-house has been placed through the ages— we have always been "immersed in secular society," and the speculations about "beyond" have been the exception rather than the norm.[11]

9 Talmud, Tractate *Avot* IV:17 (Soncino translation, p. 53).

10 See Michael Higger, *The Jewish Utopia* (Baltimore: Lord Baltimore Press, 1932); see also Arthur Lelyveld, articles "Future Life," Vol. 4, pp. 485 ff., and "Messianic Era," Vol. 7, pp. 503–504, *Universal Jewish Encyclopedia*.

11 See Abba Hillel Silver, *Where Judaism Differed* (New York: The Macmillan Company, 1957), especially Chapter XV, pp. 265 ff.

When Harvey Cox defines "secular" as ". . . taking this earthly realm, with all its health and hope, with all its sickness and sin, in utter seriousness" and punctuates that definition by an affirmation of approval, "The world becomes the horizon within which faith functions," [12] he is expressing an essentially Judaic emphasis. This is the emphasis—stressed throughout this exposition—that says that sins between man and man are heavier than sins between man and God. They are heavier and more reprehensible because they hinder *"tikkun ha-medinot"* and *"sh'lom ha-olam"*: they delay the perfecting of the nations and the peace of the world.

The relevance of this religious stance to the needs of contemporary man can be seen wherever the supreme worth of the human person is denied in practice, whether in the defoliated jungles of Vietnam or in the asphalt jungles of our Northern Negro ghettoes. These are the heavy sins between man and man that deny the Presence or turn away from it. This is the stance that calls man to the task of *kiddush hachaim,* of seeking to infuse the divine into all human relationships and allowing it to flourish in every man.

The chief inheritors of this stance are among those who are permitting it to dwindle away. Middle-class American Jews are, for the most part, suburban and at ease in Zion. Their convictions are drying up. They show widespread ignorance of the heritage; the sense that they have been given a specific role to play is fast disappearing. When prodded, they express the appropriate socially concerned opinions, but for the most part, alternating between occupation and play, they seek to convince themselves that everything is all right in this best of all possible worlds. They are not without tensions, but these are usually personal and inner tensions—the frustrations of those who have failed to "make it," the failures of interpersonal relationship, the breakthrough of a sense of emptiness, the yearning for a focus of values and for a structure of meaning.

There is relatively little evidence of the existence among them

[12] Harvey Cox, "Secularism and the Secular Mentality," *Religious Education,* Vol. LXI, No. 2 (March-April, 1966), p. 83.

of that search for integrity of self that may be at one and the same time the most fruitful effect of the major tension of our time and the dawning promise of the world's salvation. In the turbulence of our era, they are a placid backwater building inadequate dikes of material acquisitions and status charms.[13] There is tragedy in this for them and for the world. If only their sentimental affiliation could be converted into honest participation in the heritage of the Covenant People, they would find themselves and serve the larger needs of mankind. For the heritage they neglect contains the values and the meanings that are the end products of 3,300 years of Jewish experience. It possesses a beautiful—in the sense that a complex mathematical formula is aesthetically satisfying—readiness to respond to the imbalance between the obvious and the obscure movements and to accelerate the obscure movement for the redemption of our world.[14]

This is why we must look for small fellowships of the committed within the covenant community and look for allies outside, whether they remain outside or formally join the community. This attrition of values and decline of meaningful content can be halted only by a new phalanx of men and women who will take seriously the tasks imposed upon them by a demanding God; men and women who, proclaiming by their deeds that God lives, will make certain that man will live.

The need for this kind of alliance is such that it cannot exclude any who maintain the faith that humanity and humane values can survive and who commit themselves to work for it. There are those who call themselves "nontheists" or "nonbelievers" who are wholeheartedly enrolled in the task of redeem-

---

[13] Observers have marked this as a general trait of the suburban middle class. In the *Saturday Review* for June 1, 1963 (p. 13), Margaret Mead says: ". . . under nuclear threat they are walling themselves into small suburban refuges against dread and despair." I first expressed these views in an essay on "Change, Tension and the Heritage" in *The Journal of Jewish Communal Service* (Vol. XL, No. 1, Fall 1963), where I also point to the paradox of young Jews who, precisely because of their commitment to *Jewish* values, flee this kind of Jewish community in that "search for integrity."

[14] See above, Chapter Six (pp. 92–93).

ing mankind and preserving the essentially human.[15] The circle
which we draw must take them in.

We may at the same time hope that they will overcome their
inhibitions and, just as they are able to respond to the divine
Demand, that they will ultimately open themselves to the divine
Presence. This hope is generated not by any concern for the
state of their souls—they are already "saved" in their performance of the *mitzvot*—but rather by a concern for the preservation of the values that they prefer. Unless those values are anchored in enduring reality—the enduring reality we call God—
they must eventually disappear.

To believe them to be so anchored is wholly in accord with
the demands of reason. For Teilhard de Chardin, the ultimate
and purposive existent in all-that-is possesses qualities akin to
freedom and consciousness that correspond to the qualities that
are most precious in man.[16] In this kind of description of the
nature of reality, we can find the beginning of an answer to the
reductionism that lies at the base of the God-is-dead response.
It was Ludwig Feuerbach who laid the foundations of radical
theology, a century and a quarter ago, when he sought to "liber-
ate" Christianity by reducing theology to a kind of anthropology:
rejecting the God who "exists for himself" for a God who "exists
for man," thus making God relative and man absolute. This was
part of the effort of the "obscure movement" of thought to catch
up with the Copernican revolution that destroyed the possibility
of conceiving the universe in terms of an "above" and a "below."
Man who is really only "what he eats" (*"ist was er isst"*), who
is purely material, Feuerbach taught, projects what he wishes to
be—namely, Godlike—on the universe.

Says a contemporary philosophical scholar:

> It is a fundamental but seldom recognized fact that since the
> Copernican revolution theistic religion stands without a cosmol-
> ogy and is therefore forced to retreat into the domain of man's
> inwardness. Granted that even medieval language does not lack

[15] See for example, Erich Fromm, *You Shall Be As Gods* (New York:
Holt, Rinehart and Winston, Inc., 1966), especially pp. 228–229.

[16] See above, Chapter Five (p. 79).

in hints that heaven may be inside the human heart, there is still a great difference whether the image of heaven is internalized on the basis of an established cosmological correspondence or whether the internalization has no possible reference in the external order of things and thus becomes a metaphor without root.[17]

What, however, if it does have a possible reference in the external order of things? The critique that seemed adequate to the Copernican-Newtonian view of the universe no longer applies to a universe in which space and time, size, and distance have been shattered. Again, we are lagging. Teilhard de Chardin's closely reasoned description of evolution as the development of ever-greater refinement of consciousness, conscious of itself, supports the view that there is not only a "possible reference" but an identity between man's emergent consciousness and cosmic "primacy." He writes:

> Man is not the center of the universe as once we thought in our simplicity, but something much more wonderful—the arrow pointing the way to the final unification of the world in terms of life . . .
> Mankind was a fragile and even fictitious construction so long as it could only have a limited, plural and disjointed cosmos as setting; but it becomes consistent and at the same time probable as soon as it is brought within the compass of a biological space-time and appears as a continuation of the very lines of the universe amongst other realities as vast as itself.[18]

We need no psychedelic, LSD-type escapes when we plunge into the revelations of the new physical sciences. The mind-stretching revelations of which they hint do the reverse of *reducing* the cosmic to the human. They *expand* our horizons by leading us to see the relationship between what we internalize and the wondrous and exciting thrust of that Whole of which we are

[17] Jacob Taubes, "The Copernican Turn of Theology," in *Religious Experience and Truth,* ed. Sidney Hook (New York: New York University Press, 1961), p. 73.
[18] Pierre Teilhard de Chardin, *The Phenomenon of Man* (New York: Harper & Row, 1961), pp. 223, 246.

part and into which we are granted occasional soul-stirring glimpses.

This is what leads an eminent American paleontologist and anthropologist to ask the question, "How natural is natural?" [19] We have already stated our conviction that all-that-is is "natural"; but what depths of intricacy and wonder are contained in that simple designation. Loren Eiseley, writing of the effort to create "life" in the laboratory, opens the door to that wonder. "We shall have great need of humbleness," on the day we succeed, he says.

> As for me, if I am still around on that day, I intend to put on my old hat and climb over the wall as usual. . . . I will wonder, as always, in what manner "particles" pursue such devious plans and symmetries. I will ask once more in what way it is managed, that the simple dust takes on a history and begins to weave these unique and never recurring apparitions in the stream of time. . . .
>
> I do not think, if someone finally twists the key successfully in the tiniest and most humble house of life, that many of these questions will be answered, or that the dark forces which create lights in the deep sea and living batteries in the waters of tropical swamps, or the dread cycles of parasites, or the most noble workings of the human brain, will be much if at all revealed. Rather, I would say that if "dead" matter has reared up this curious landscape of fiddling crickets, song sparrows, and wondering men, it must be plain even to the most devoted materialist that the matter of which he speaks contains amazing, if not dreadful powers, and may not impossibly be, as Hardy has suggested, "but one mask of many worn by the Great Face behind." [20]

This is more than scientific humility; it is a capacity to appreciate the color and variety of the miraculous physical world of which we are part, which is more true than the truths of the prosy language choppers, who see only functioning parts and miss the address of the larger scheme. That scheme's development must have more in store for us than the reduction of human life to factors in the environment of the machine. Those

[19] Loren Eiseley, *The Firmament of Time* (New York: Atheneum, 1960), pp. 150–181.

[20] *The Immense Journey* (New York: Random House, 1957), pp. 208 ff.

who embrace the supposed consequents of dynamic technology, who fragmentize music, art, the word, and life itself, should know what it is that they frustrate by their limited view of the canons of human reasoning.[21] They frustrate the full development of man, demean his potentiality, and threaten him with failure as the topmost vertical on the tree of evolution—the failure of vital creativity, of self-conscious direction toward profounder, more fully formed consciousness. Man dehumanized will degenerate into mechanism, a directed robot rather than a self-directing being. Only when man is fully man can the preeminently human—reflection and its expression in language and other symbolic forms—become more and more luminous.

This frustration of potential would be only *our* tragedy. Even if we destroy this planet, as we seem capable of doing, it would *not* mean the end of the enterprise. The universe is vast. If we throw away our birthright, miss this opportunity, then the ever-burgeoning spiral of evolution will throw off some new experiment.

But *our* tragedy is enough for us. Deep within us, stronger even than the will to meaning, is the will to meaningful accomplishment. It is not enough to be what we are; we must become what we are capable of becoming. To know that we may do so, that we may align ourselves with the purpose of all life, that we may be co-workers with God, is the solid foundation for the structure of meaning we need so desperately.

A conviction of ultimate meaning is the product of the action that is itself intended to fulfill it. It is like falling in love—you respond, you seek, you do—you do not sit down to reason it out. I have learned that it is not possible to lead people intellectually into a structure of meaning, any more than it is possible to convince a young person by reasoned argument that this or that person of the opposite sex is the one "destined" for him.

Each of us must win his own way. This book is but a reflection of the effort of one individual to do so. I can but state my convictions. You must find your own.

[21] See above, Chapter Three.

This is the structure to which I have come—not without doubt, not without struggle, not without pain:

I am convinced that there exists at the heart of the universe,[22] more real than any reality we can conceive, a consciousness akin to our own consciousness, but of which we can have but a fragmentary and inadequate intuition—"as through a glass, darkly"—even though in it our individual consciousness has its being.

I am convinced that at the heart of the universe there is a sympathy akin to our sympathy, responding to our striving, but so far beyond our capacity to understand that we can but touch the hem of it.

I am convinced that at the heart of the universe there is a love akin to our love, but that of it, that which we brokenly call "love" is but a pale and limited reflection.

I am convinced that the long, painful, upward evolution of life has been marked by a development—rudimentary and primitive as it is at its present stage—of that consciousness, that sympathy, and that love.

I am convinced that we can experience, in what I have described as a sense of Presence, the reality of that consciousness, sympathy, and love; that we can stand in relationship to that Presence and that this is what men have striven toward when they have said "God."

I am convinced that this ultimate reality that we call God makes demands upon man, and indeed, infused into all-that-is, makes demands upon all existence; that the primary demand of God is the establishment of *Kedusha,* the Divine Presence, in all life and all relationships; that this Presence is the ever-growing refinement of consciousness, sympathy, and love.

I am convinced that our values can be grounded in this Demand, that the good can be defined in terms of the relationship of our actions to the enhancement of consciousness, sympathy, and love.

[22] I use the phrase "heart of the universe" metaphorically, not spatially or implying any category of position.

I am convinced that the new knowledge that the second-quarter of the twentieth century has produced has given us insights into the unity and purposiveness of our universe that make it more difficult than ever before to deny God and to view absurdity and despair as the character of being; that from the standpoint of a search for a viable world-outlook it must be affirmed that God lives.

My structure of meaning includes, necessarily, a conviction about the meaningfulness of my own identity. As a Jew, I participate in convictions that are particularistic in that they define the role of the covenant community. These convictions do not shut out the universal. Rather, they invite its fellowship, in whatever form it may express itself and with whatever words it may be verbalized, in that shared struggle to establish the human manifestations of consciousness and sympathy and love, to constitute the affirmation of God's kingship.

Thus, I am convinced that the history of the people of Israel has as its significant distinctive mark—out of primitive beginnings to blazing and revolutionary insights, uneven, fallible, frustrated again and again, but persisting—the quest for an understanding of that consciousness, that sympathy, and that love and for its establishment among men.

Out of that history have risen soaring geniuses in the realm of relationship—from the prophets of old to an Einstein of our day, reverently exploring the utmost physical frontiers and beautifully symbolizing in his life the meaning of love, to a Martin Buber, penetrating with his poetic insight the spiritual frontiers and casting up in the wilderness a way to the meeting of man with man.

Through that history, I as an individual am not only part of mankind but part of a covenant folk—a folk that has at rare and glorious moments deserved the appellation *"rachmonim b'nai rachmonim*—compassionate children of compassionate parents."

But these are words, not a structure of meaning. To become a structure, they must be built into our lives in functioning relationships with men and with the source of meaning. This requires the cultivation of a skill: to be able to release "the seven iron bands about our heart," to learn to open ourselves to the Presence in our fellow men, in mankind and its goals, in the cosmos with its unfulfilled destiny. This is the skill that is prerequisite to hearing the demand of God and to the joy of responding in action.

It is a skill that can be learned. It is both simple and difficult—as simple and as difficult as it was two and a half millennia ago when the prophet Jeremiah (29:13) said: "And ye shall seek Me, and find Me, when ye shall search for Me with all your heart."

INDEX

Abba b. Kahana, Rabbi (3rd century), 138
abracadabra, 115
address and response, 159, 167–168
Adler, Alfred (1870–1937), 27
agnosticism, 90–91
Akiba, Rabbi, 52, 180
alienation, 26
all-that-is, 10–11, 120–121, 129, 131, 181, 196
Altizer, Thomas J. J., 35, 50–52, 62
Amos, 31
Anders, Günther, 154
anomie, 26
anonymity, 38–39
apikoros, 13
Arnold, Matthew (1822–1888), 98
art, 21–22, 82
astrology, 112
atheism, vii, 7, 12, 85, 91
  Marxist, 86
  practical form of, 13–14
Attila (406?–453), 174
Auschwitz, 109–110, 117, 172, 175, 181
automation, 16
axiologists, 163–164

Babel, Tower of, 43–44

Bar Kochba, Simon (died 135), 180
b'di-avad, 53
Beecher, Henry Ward (1813–1887), 186
belief
  contrasted with action, 159
  in nothing, 189
  subjective character of, 158
Belshazzar, 32
Ben Azzai, Simon (1st century), 136
Bennett, Charles A. (1885–1930), 156
Berdichever Rebbe, viii, 180
Berdyaev, Nicolas (1874–1948), 22
Betar, 180–181
Bible criticism, 77
Black Plague, 173
blik, 73
Bohr, Niels (1885–1962), 122
Bonhoeffer, Dietrich (1906–1945), 34, 57, 59
Bozell, Brent, 190
b'racha, 137
b'rit, 159
Broude, William G., 103
Browning, Robert (1812–1889), 156
Bruce, Alexander B. (1831–1899), 177

201